sense /sɛn(t)s/

verb

• to feel to be conscious of: *all the raised felicities that human nature is capable of sensing.*

• to have a sense perception of (an object, occurrence, etc.). Also occasionally: to be aware of having (a sensation); *intransitive*: to experience sensations: *we did not then* perceive *extension or space as such, although it was* felt *in the very first breath which consciousness drew, and was afterward* sensed.

• of a machine, instrument, or similar device: to detect or to measure: *the discovery of a method for sensing and locating macroseisms through the body of the planet.*

Oxford English Dictionary, 3rd Edition

IN THIS ISSUE

LA+ SENSE EDITORIAL

More and more technologies are being created to sense our environment, and much is being learned about how animals and plants sense theirs. We often think of these tools as extending our capacity for sensing what is not available through natural human perception. But what is natural about perception? Though our senses have a biological basis, they are not simply intermediaries through which we gain empirical knowledge about our world. How do senses become naturalized, and bodies and experiences standardized?

We begin this issue with an essay on the sense of self by philosopher Mark Kingwell, who considers the essential metaphysical question: How do we know what we know? If our sense organs are not simply receptors, can we (or should we) trust them? The next grouping of essays provides historical examples of how our senses become "naturalized." Using the case study of mineral waters, landscape architect Sarah Coleman describes how shared meanings of taste grow out of place-based rituals. As global markets capitalize on the "taste of place" through transportable products, the connection to the landscape is lost. Historian Ai Hisano likewise describes how the standardization of food colors helped to educate consumers about the proper "naturalness" of food, whereby an individual's sensation was no longer considered subjective but something to be scientifically understood and mass-produced. Of course, not all can be explained scientifically, as the essay by anthropologist Jia Hui Lee elucidates. Citing experiments with rats, "witches," and the art of perfumery, Lee shows how smell–the sense most closely linked to memory–remains a mystery due to the gap between olfactory science and the experience of odors. Nevertheless, we each have a unique odor, as distinct as a fingerprint. This fact can be used for far less benign purposes than perfumery, as art historian/curator Elena Giulia Abbiatici shows. Increasingly sophisticated surveillance technologies raise many ethical issues that are being illuminated in compelling and disturbing projects by various artists.

Sensing for surveillance is not limited to the human sensorium. Media theorist Lisa Yin Han considers the US military's analysis of marine species' communication signals. The soundscapes produced by these living sensors are studied for anomalies to detect possible foreign watercraft. Han asks how we might develop a multispecies "common sense" beyond one of top-down control. Landscape architect and geographer Douglas Robb's essay pays tribute to his frequent collaborator and *LA+ GEO* co-author, Karen Bakker. Robb describes how the sounds of life made audible through digital sensing have opened a world of wonder, offering lessons for landscape architects, including the importance of deep listening. Similarly, *LA+* spoke with artist Mark Peter Wright about slow listening, the ethics of field recording, and how to listen for things we cannot hear. Anthropologist David Howes reminds us of the diversity and richness of "sensory cosmologies" across cultures and urges designers to resist ocularcentrism by embracing the full spectrum of sensory experiences.

The next grouping of essays considers how technology, methods of measure, and subsequent standardization of bodies can lead to exclusionary practices. Using the case study of early smog detection in Los Angeles, Erin Putalik and Sally Pusede describe how increasing instrumentation for measuring smog led to important environmental regulations, but it eventually granted authority to mechanical devices over embodied experiences, obscuring the uneven distribution of pollution and ongoing struggles for environmental justice. Artist/curator Chris Salter considers the longstanding desire for ubiquitous computing to "liberate" the body from technology such that the distinction among humans, technologies, and environments collapses. Salter asks us to consider what kinds of bodies are being considered when developing this technology. Writing about the experience of exclusion from her personal experiences as a Deaf person, landscape architect Alexa Vaughn argues that the design disciplines and laws have far to go toward making places and spaces that are inclusive of a wide range of sense-abilities. Exclusionary practices through sense-making apply not only to individuals but to neighborhoods and cities. Sonic theorist and musician Gascia Ouzounian writes about the emergence of noise mapping as industrialization and urbanization rapidly increased. While noise regulations help protect residents from unhealthy decibel levels, Ouzounian discusses how such regulations can be used in the service of gentrification. Geographer Tim Cresswell similarly shows how noise and smells can be used to celebrate a sense of place or, alternately, framed as negative in the service of erasing places deemed undesirable by some.

We conclude this issue with two essays about the importance of creative works for sensitizing our imagination toward future possibilities. Author and media studies scholar Alexa Weik von Mossner describes the power of writers and filmmakers to evoke multisensory environments in ways that allow us to feel what different futures might be like. Art historian Kris Paulsen asks us to consider different conceptions of time altogether. Weaving together science fiction, NASA rover missions, and the captivating ceramics and tapestries created by Sarah Rosalena, Paulsen argues that spiraling "timeslips" unsettle notions of linear time, directing our attention away from futures chosen by tech entrepreneurs and bending our view back down to Earth.

Karen M'Closkey
Issue Editor

SENSE-CERTAINTY, IDENTITY, AND THE REALITY PARADOX

>MARK KINGWELL

SENSE-CERTAINTY, IDENTITY, AND THE REALITY PARADOX
MARK KINGWELL

Mark Kingwell is a professor of philosophy at the University of Toronto and a contributing editor of *Harper's Magazine* in New York. He is the author of many books and articles on politics, art, design, and architecture. His most recent book is *Singular Creatures: Robots, Rights, and the Politics of Posthumanism* (2022).

+ LITERATURE, PHILOSOPHY

Philosophy, the love of wisdom, has often been considered impossible, usually for reasons having to do with how people we dislike go about doing it. Philosophers are forever in the business of putting each other out of business. The typical charges involve malfeasance, confusion, muddled thinking, and dangerous metaphysical tendencies. It is a surprise only to those outside the profession that the presumptively mild-mannered pursuit of clarity in thought should be so inherently murderous.

Most of these internecine disputes can be managed, or understood, by way of sufficient distance (who cares?) or dialectical ingenuity (I absorb your limited view *thus*!). What cannot be so salved is the enduring damage of the *basic paradox of all philosophy*, the serpent coiled in its heart. By this I mean philosophy's reliance on a picture of reality that is rooted in sensory experience. This picture, no matter its complexity, is afflicted by an apparently insuperable intellectual pincer movement, a skeptical double-flank collapse. How can understanding understand itself without replicating the sensory errors of any understanding? I therefore want to pose a philosophical question about the senses that has implications for everything from art to politics to fashion, and every stop in between. It is this: Can the senses ever save us from the lurking monster of metaphysical doubt?

Consider, on the one hand, the fact that most philosophers set themselves up as arbiters of reality, adjudicating against misleading appearances. This is how Plato began and how most of us still go on. On the other hand, and at the very same time, erecting this basic distinction between what appears and what is real seems to cleave ourselves and the world in an irretrievable way. Descartes or Kant can call on sensory deceptions as a caution against epistemological complacency, but only in the service of a larger metaphysics that kicks the problem down the road. Retrieved reality, shorn of deceptive appearances, is just as susceptible to doubt as optical illusions, lies, *trompe l'oeil* japes, and the like. Restored reality, the educated sensorium, will not save us.

One of the few philosophers to take this endgame seriously was Ludwig Wittgenstein, together with his long-distance disciple, the American Stanley Cavell. "A picture held us captive," Wittgenstein tells us in *Philosophical Investigations*. "And we could not get outside it, for it lay in our language and language seemed to repeat it to us inexorably."[1] So it did, and so it does. But it is more than language that is at fault here; it is sensory life itself, our too-troubled immersion in the *son et lumière* of worldly existence. And yet, what can we do about it? Discarding one picture seems only to invite replacement by another distinguished only by its self-congratulation at not being the first. Cavell will suggest a discipline of endless acknowledgment. In this essay, I take up that challenge and assess its viability as a response to the paradox of philosophy. Can we still believe our eyes? Or must we, metaphorically at least, pluck them from their sockets in a paroxysm of Biblical disgust? Or is it, somehow, both?

This kind of questioning leads, in turn, to some puzzles that are as familiar in the history of philosophy as they are in science fiction: Descartes's malicious demon, the brain-in-the-vat thought experiment, the *Matrix's* red pill versus blue pill choice, the so-called Experience Machine, and so on. All of them have been brought up to date by emerging technologies that suggest an unsettling possibility: could we be, right now, part of a vast computer simulation and yet not know it? The epistemo-action thriller is by now an accepted genre within speculative fiction, especially film, with its ability to create immersive experiences. These cinematic exercises in perception-bending and unreliable context are often called postmodern, but in fact their cognitive commitments are decisively modern, if not premodern. They are, that is to say, preoccupied with the ancient appearance/reality distinction and with ways of securing a foundation for our apparently unstable experience of the modern world.

The appearance/reality exercise becomes decisively modern with the subjects' focus on their own consciousness, attempting to put the experience of experience itself into critical view. The Cartesian attempt is significant not only because it spawns so much later reflection and reaction, but also because Descartes at once poses the problem in a way that makes it seem insoluble even as he claims to solve it.

Once again, how do we know anything at all? Descartes is confident that if we adopt a method of hyperbolic doubt, questioning every aspect and level of what we take to be true, we can isolate something beyond doubt. This is, as everyone knows, the celebrated *cogito*–I think–which underwrites its equally famous *ergo sum* supplement: therefore I am. This does not mean that only thinking beings are truly alive, or that we are most vital when thinking – two common misinterpretations. It means, rather, that the act of thinking itself proves the existence of something, namely the *res cogitans* or thinking thing which a conscious subject essentially is.

Technologist, off-world colonizer, and sometimes *Simpsons* character Elon Musk is merely the most recent to articulate the radical idea that we are living in a vast computer simulation run by future versions of ourselves. The "simulation argument," developed by philosopher Nick Bostrom, argues that, given the nature of computer power and its presumed ability to affect and even replicate human consciousness, it is overwhelmingly likely that we are within one of millions of such simulations. We are Sims and we do not know it![2] The claim is striking both for its logical elegance and for its ability to rattle the cage of ordinary mortals. Like debates about free will and determinism, the simulation argument takes our unique sense of self, our hopes, desires, and halting actions, and renders them null. No wonder the scenario is old, even if the computer-based argument is new. The gods toy with us as wanton boys play with flies, but now the gods are made of tin.

In current circumstances, the simulation argument dovetails with a worry born of more practical struggles in the world of politics: if your previously rock-solid reality as a unique consciousness is undermined by this contingency, then why not by others? The tricky crosscurrents of identity politics, where conflicting claims of status and value hinge on race, orientation, ability, or history, might prove to be the birthplace of a world without individuals. Technologists will tell you the posthuman future is inevitable, maybe already here, and that they joyously await the Singularity (where non-human intelligence outstrips our slow biological brains). Most of us are more cautious, not least because we know that the future is always unevenly distributed and that the adapt-or-die cheerfulness of tech boosters too often conceals drastic structural inequalities.

There are human limits that are not about mortality but are a function of human relations. Claims of political status based on identity have always been advanced to challenge structural asymmetries: exclusions driven by skin color, differences in genital arrangement, differences in desire. This is the rankest stupidity. There is a tangle here, as intersectionality advocates well know. If your claims to status are based on reversing this kind of discrimination, you run the risk of making the difference itself–rather than the claim to status–the political focal point. Identity politics aims for a day when all individuals are valued in themselves, but those aspects of unique individuality that have been systematically denigrated can, paradoxically, become barriers to the achievement of individual value.

Imagine, then, a world in which people do not define themselves by their various clusters of traits or get to claim privileges based upon them. It would also be a world in which some cluster of traits was no longer cause for discrimination or violence. In metaphysical terms, the problem here is not the differential treatment of traits, but the fact that traits are clustered in the first place, forming individuals who are supposed to be both different and the same. The political threshold here is the persistent idea of the individual as unique and self-identical. Born in struggles against hierarchy and religious intolerance some four centuries ago (in the West at least), the social-political individual has led a rocky life. It has borne property rights and generated social revolution, but it has also declined into mere consumer preference or Twitter-Instagram-TikTok presence.

In a world without individuals, the uniqueness of my consciousness would not signify much, nor would its possibilities ever be constrained by being tied to a stable identity. The "I" of my personal narrative would acknowledge its own fictional status, a minimal ordering principle as it runs one experiment in human living after another. Discrimination would be rendered incoherent. In a post-individual world, we would really be running the simulations ourselves, using bodies and the material world as test benches. This would be a posthuman world, unrecognizable to most of what currently counts as human life. These are the real metaphysical stakes of loosening the moorings of selfhood. The simulation argument forces imagination to confront its own mysteries, but it does little to advance the issue. Meanwhile, we seem trapped in a different kind of snare, one that is not speculative at all.

The human present is mired in prejudice and evil, apparently basic circumstances against which the best efforts of identity-based empowerment have been only moderately successful. The human future seems to promise more of the same, only with the unpleasant kicker that we will find new, possibly worse ways of extending inequality by heeding "what technology wants." Is there another way? Could we fashion a world in which differences really were transcended, where nobody was worth more or less than anyone else, where the ultimate value was not individual identity but the multiplicity of unlikely meet-minds, windowless mirrors each reflecting all the others, making things up? That is the idea of justice, it seems to me. And while it can sometimes seem like a haunting dream rather than any sort of proximate possibility, I believe we must continue to think and act as if it is within reach.

There will always be trouble, of course, because "we" remain suspended somewhere between mind and world. How can this thinking thing that I consider the locus of my identity be conjoined in some smooth continuous sense? With, furthermore, a physical body that is itself just part of the material world: *res extensa*, or extended things in space?

My favorite exchange about the problem occurs in a play, not in a philosophy treatise. The play is about a play that has a play nestled within it, and it puts at its center two characters from the original play who are hapless minor playthings of fortune.[3] The key passage for me starts this way.

Guildenstern (for it is he) is confused and provoked by his predicament. "But for God's sake what are we supposed to do?!" The desperate cry is addressed to a mysterious jester-like figure called the Player. He is the leader of a troupe of actors headed to the original play's main action, there to catch the conscience of the king. "Relax," advises the Player. "Respond. That's what people do. You can't go through life questioning your situation at every turn."

This is no help to Guildenstern. "But we don't know what's going on, or what to do with ourselves," he wails, as we so often want to do. "We don't know how to act." The Player is suave in response, like unhelpful advisors everywhere from guidance offices to therapy sessions. "Act natural," he says. You imagine him smiling in a gently mocking way. "You know why you're here at least." But Guildenstern does not know any such thing. "We only know what we're told, and that's little enough. And for all we know it isn't even true." The Player pounces on this, the basic difficulty. "For all anyone knows, nothing is," he tells the doomed henchman in the same soothing tones. "Everything has to be taken on trust; truth is only that which is taken to be true. It's the currency of living." A pause here, I think, to let all these ideas sink in a bit. This is a long speech for the Player. "There may be nothing behind it," he goes, conceding what might be thought a minor point from his attitude, "but it doesn't make any difference so long as it is honoured. One acts on assumptions. What do you assume?"

It does not make any difference so long as it is honored. But is that true? Is that the only final truth about truth? And all this is excellent-sounding life-player advice, but does it help very much? Don't know how to act? Act natural! Don't know what to do? Relax! Respond! Truth? Just what is taken to be true. Trust your assumptions! This may well make one a player, or even a Player. But is it enough to be going on with?

No, do not trust your assumptions – at least not all the time. Put those assumptions into question over and over, one by one. You cannot get outside the circle of assumptions any

more than you can eliminate all prejudice. These are the only possible foundations of knowledge. They are shaky but necessary. Descartes was right: take out one apple at a time to see if any of them are rotten. But he was also wrong: you cannot remove all the apples to examine the basket, because the basket is you, and you are the one assessing the apples. My own view is that God will not help you here. Even on most sympathetic accounts, He probably has larger concerns than whether your sense impressions align with the world.[4] But, by the same token, it also seems highly unlikely that there is a malicious demon or a supercomputer generating the whole scene of experience. And if I am wrong about either possibility, well, it does not seem to matter much inside the scene.

Guildenstern is frustrated by being suspended inside the scene this way. To him, there always seems to be a play within the play, or a sense that he is trapped inside a story that is not his own. And so, he asks, prayerfully, "All I ask is our common clue, give us this day our daily cue." Elsewhere, matters are even more fraught: "Give us this day our daily mask." At yet another point and, even more poignantly, "Give us this day our daily week."

Cue, mask, time. Not even the almighty can make a day into a week or provide more than clues about how to be here, when how includes why. No. We have to figure that out for ourselves; and sometimes, maybe all too often, we will find ourselves at sea with no orders forthcoming. If only we had a clue, a cue, anything!

Be careful what you wish for. In such a state of doubt, it is not only minor characters who cannot master the world with knowledge. You might be the mighty one who finds a trifle, a stray handkerchief, that tears the world asunder. When Othello is confronted by Desdemona's personal item, a gift he has given her after receiving it from his own mother, we already know that things have gone wrong. They are about to get worse. Othello is a tragic figure in a way that requires no immersive technology or off-world appearance machine. Paradoxically, he deceives himself precisely because he wants to believe. Here the will to believe meets the trace of the real, because it is, in fact, her handkerchief – it is not a fake, or a duplicate, though there is a suggestion that one might be part of the overall plot. But its coming to be in Cassio's lodging has all the makings of a tragic Gettier case. It is Desdemona's cherished present, a sign of Othello's love and her fidelity; we are told that she keeps it always with her, to "kiss and talk to." She tried to use it to soothe Othello's headache. And yet, the play hints that Othello's mother got it from a sorceress, and certainly he is ensorcelled by its presence.

We know that Iago has planted the handkerchief. Othello does not. And, effectively primed by Iago's bilious counsel and, alas, his own proclivity to jealously, he accepts the proffered sign. He believes he has justified true belief about Desdemona's infidelity. Iago has made the main point in a smug soliloquy about Othello's credulity: "Trifles light as air / Are to the jealous confirmations strong / As proofs of holy writ." When a person is murderously jealous, it doesn't take much *evidence* to set them off. Usually seen as a plaything of runaway presuppositions, namely his awful willingness to entertain suspicions about Desdemona, Othello is actually a victim of misplaced empiricism. He demanded proof, and so proof was provided. The tragedy is not Iago's deception, but rather Othello's combination of distrust and willingness to believe. He is double-tapped, by skepticism and authority alike. Worst of all, he does it to himself.

The resulting scene is among the most wrenching in English literature. Othello's murder of Desdemona is hard to watch. In the last production I saw, the director decided to extend the strangling for as long as such a violent act might take in real life. It was harrowing. In the row in front of me, a burly man wearing a lumberjack shirt and a trucker cap–not an image of the effete theater-goer–sat there with tears streaming down his face, eyes locked on the stage. I felt like throwing up myself.

Never in my life have I experienced so powerfully the peculiar leverage of aesthetic distance, that voluntary-but-not-really-voluntary principle that keeps us in our seats when every moral fiber is urging us to rush the stage and prevent the disastrous outcome. We call this "willingness suspension of disbelief," but there is something pretty unwilling about it at extreme moments such as this. Intellectually we mock the idea of the yokel rushing the stage to try and explain what is really happening. We feel so pinned to our seats because, in part, our fear and pity are real. We need to feel these emotions, but ideally in controlled environments. Aristotle knew this when he wrote about tragic catharsis. What is fiction except a series of wrenching, compelling thought experiments? The pressing questions of knowledge and action are here forever renewed and revitalized.

How do we acknowledge the otherness of the other?[5] The yokel who rushes the stage is not wrong, just mistaken – there is a difference. And we? What do we do? Well, we may never take handkerchiefs for granted again. And we might wonder, when knowledge seems so secure, whether our justification is really as iron-clad as we imagine.

I have not forgotten about the second, general paradox of philosophy. It is this: you can only see the value of thinking philosophically when you are already doing it. Before that, philosophical thinking will seem useless, contrived, self-contradictory, and hopelessly vague. It is almost its own bad-luck Gettier problem: the clock of thought has stopped telling practical time, and though it is right twice a day for purely adventitious reasons, it is not tracking reality. Except, except – there is something that even a hostile or bored student glimpses in this otherwise strange way of going on. Maybe she recalls the childish questions that were put away as time went by: When I see blue, do I see the same thing you do? When I fall asleep, where does my mind go? Why is it okay to eat cows but not to eat my cat?

Socrates knew that the only way to get someone to think philosophically was to capture their imagination. You cannot argue someone into it, because its value is only evident to those whose values have altered under its influence. Not even reason is sufficient to self-prove the value of reason. And, though it may be comforting and apparently certain, revelation is no better option. That which only I can see is not, by definition, scalable or falsifiable. It does not translate.

1 Ludwig Wittgenstein, *Philosophical Investigations*, trans. G. E. M. Anscombe (Blackwell, 1953), para. 115.

2 Nick Bostrom, "Are You Living in a Computer Simulation?" *Philosophical Quarterly* 53, no. 211 (2003): 243–55. To be more precise than my quick summary: "This paper argues that at least one of the following propositions is true: (1) the human species is very likely to go extinct before reaching a 'posthuman' stage; (2) any posthuman civilization is extremely unlikely to run a significant number of simulations of their evolutionary history (or variations thereof); (3) we are almost certainly living in a computer simulation. It follows that the belief that there is a significant chance that we will one day become posthumans who run ancestor-simulations is false, unless we are currently living in a simulation." The idea here is to fork (or tri-fork) the available choices so that we are forced to accept the otherwise unprovable (and maybe unpalatable) possible conclusion.

3 Tom Stoppard, *Rosencrantz and Guildenstern Are Dead* (1966).

4 Notice posted in a French church: "When you enter this church it may be possible that you hear 'the call of God'. However, it is unlikely that he will call you on your mobile. Thank you for turning off your phones. If you want to talk to God, enter, choose a quiet place and talk to him. If you want to see Him, send Him a text while driving."

5 This is the perennial query of the philosopher Stanley Cavell, whose reading of *Othello* has shaped my thoughts about the play and much else. See Cavell, *The Claim of Reason: Wittgenstein, Skepticism, Morality, and Tragedy* (Oxford University Press, 1999) and *Disowning Knowledge in Seven Plays of Shakespeare* (Cambridge University Press, 2003).

SARAH COLEMAN

TASTING THE CURE

Sarah Coleman is an assistant professor of landscape architecture at Auburn University and the program director for the department's study abroad program in Tbilisi. During 2021–22, she was a Fulbright student scholar in Borjomi, Georgia, where she explored the potential of new interpretive design strategies in the historic health landscapes on and around the Sadgeri Plateau.

+ ADVERTISING, HEALTH

On thedeepestsite.com, a visitor is invited to journey, in increments of a mouse's scroll wheel, the full 8,000-meter distance into the earth to the origin of the Caucasus's most iconic mineral water.[1] Naturally infused with carbon dioxide, this water surfaces in the central Georgian town of Borjomi absent any mechanical intervention. Dissolving small amounts of minerals as it presses upward through layers of volcanic rock, this journey, according to the producer and distributor of the brand, is encoded in the water's taste. Its strong, earthy, slightly salty flavor indexes the region's ancient volcanic origins, drawing upon the mystery of that which is not seen, a product of deep geologic time. A recent advertisement goes so far as to suggest that these are "juvenile waters," "new" waters that have never entered the earth's hydrologic cycle.[2]

This story of the water's primordial origins perhaps attempts to toe a semantic line between its newer Euro-American markets, who expect "purity" (i.e., tastelessness), and its original audience, for whom the highly mineral flavor still motivates the act of its drinking. It signals the water's fortifying and even *medicinal* properties.[3] That is, those drinking Borjomi in the former Soviet Republics expect "to get something out of" the water. Relative to the transparence of "pure" drinking waters, that *something*–here, a solution of dissolved bicarbonates, chlorides, calcium, magnesium, sodium, and potassium–affords a mineral and semantic surface onto which meanings are strategically inscribed.

For an individual human body, the sense of taste and, to some degree, its close cousin, smell, are distinct amongst the traditionally delineated five senses in that they index a material passage across the corporeal boundaries of outside and inside. The act of tasting immediately precedes absorption and metabolism, while the experience of smell is inseparable from respiration. These essential life processes involve the incorporation of matter into the body. However, taste might also be understood as a social sense wherein *shared meanings of taste* are socio-culturally constructed, inscribed, and performed.[4] In other words, what something "tastes *like*" is mutable and unsettled, dependent upon and changing within a particular context or place.

Taste of Place

On April 29, 2022, two months after the Russian invasion of Ukraine, IDS Borjomi suspended operations at both of its mineral water bottling plants. Citing sanctions imposed by Western governments, the majority Russian-owned conglomerate explained that its export sales to 40 countries had become impossible. Employees were required to sign new contracts for half their usual salaries, stoking long held and ever-present Georgian enmity against the aggressor to the north. Russia currently occupies 20% of Georgia, a result of violent territorial wars in 1992 and 2008, prompting parallels to the conflict in Ukraine. "Borjomi has been exported and sold as a Russian product," explained Otar Abesadze, a professor of economics at Tbilisi State University. "This is a huge insult to Georgian identity and one of the biggest failures of our government."[5]

Workers at the plant–mostly residents of the municipality–initiated a strike, resulting in thousands of liters of the iconic Georgian mineral water being diverted into the

Gujaretitskali River each day. After a month-long impasse, sanctioned oligarch Mikhail Fridman offered 8% of his stake in Borjomi to the Georgian government at no cost. This rebalanced the majority ownership in Georgia's favor, which currently controls 51% of the share to Russia's 49%.[6]

Immediately, the new Georgian majority set about reterritorializing the water. A 2023 commercial reimagines the Borjomi legend, where a hunter chases a wounded deer into a dark conifer wood.[7] He witnesses it drink from a spring that miraculously heals its injuries. Though the story of the water's discovery typically ends here, the ad follows the hunter as he carries the water across Georgia, sharing it with his countrymen, encountering every bit of UNESCO-endorsed landscape and postcard-ready "intangible cultural heritage" along the way. In the High Caucasus Mountains, the taste of the water inspires Tushetian shepherds to perform an acrobatic dance in traditional Sukhishvili-style (the beloved national ballet), leaping along a ridgeline in their woolen *paphki* hats and long *chokha* tunics. The hunter arrives in a medieval-ish Kartlian market square, shaded by the classical conic dome of a Georgian Orthodox church, where he offers a revitalizing drink to two wrestlers engaged in the chivalric martial art of *chidaoba*. Suddenly, the scene shifts to the present day, where contemporary Tbilisians take flight over the posh Vake neighborhood as they taste Borjomi. In this telling, the water unifies the nation across time and geography, a collective patrimony, and an essential source of Georgian cultural vitality.

The combination of the unique biophysical properties of a landscape (soil, microclimate, and native plants, for example) and the cultural practices that have contributed to the development and evolution of particular foods, waters, and flavors are central to concepts of *terroir*, "the taste of place."[8] Yet, each of these narratives of Borjomi's taste—the hydrogeologic, the mythical, the nationalist—share in common a distancing from the precise point of origin of the water—the real place in which it surfaces—and evade any allusion to the historic "tasting activities" that initially imbued it with its healthful status.[9] Perhaps one thing Georgians and Russians can currently agree upon: that dredging up Russo-imperial or Soviet pasts is unpalatable, or at least unmarketable.

Acts of Incorporation

Borjomi itself is only one of a cluster of towns and villages that once comprised the Caucasus's most famous *kurort* ("cure place"), territories set aside across the Soviet Union as sites of exchange between the human body and the curative properties embedded within a landscape. Due to its mild alpine climate and the number and diversity of mineral springs that emerged from its volcanic plateaus and river valleys, the region situated amidst the low mountains of the Trialeti Range was known as the "Pearl of the Caucasus." During the 19th century, these waters were taken as "cure-alls" by the Russian imperial elite. However, in the Soviet period, as expert chemists and physicians were increasingly charged with the conservation and management of these territories, the chemical properties of each spring became associated with precise treatments for specific ailments.[10] Variations in taste and smell evidenced each spring's distinct healing properties which were to be taken at their source—ensuring the stability of the dose—in the prescribed volume and frequency.[11]

These waters are not conventionally delicious; for the uninitiated, their taste is jarring, even unpleasant. Yet cultural tastes can frame physiological taste experiences so intensely that even what does not afford "naked pleasure" may nonetheless appeal to our "dressed taste."[12] In other words, the twin actions of tasting *and* thinking (engaging our cultural beliefs) might convert a flavor that does not provide hedonic pleasure into something that "tastes good," as in "good *for* us," "nourishing," or even "medicinal." To illustrate, the ferrous mineral springs that emerged near the village Tsaghveri were well-known for their curative influence on diseases of the respiratory organs, gastroenteric tracts, and anemia.[13] Though apparently crystalline, the black basalt fountain at the center of the village park is stained red-orange with efflorescences that cake into chalky patinas and flake off into its basin. A stainless-steel pipe sucks in air as water is displaced from the spring chamber, emitting a continuous, low whistle that implies a vast depth below. Drawing the water toward the nose and mouth, it smells of blood and sulfur. It tastes this way too, but also of soil and iron. As it meets the tongue, carbon dioxide bubbles roil across the palette and unsettle the sensitive hairs of the nasal passage. The taste of rust remains in the throat and nose long after the water has been swallowed. The sensorial intensity of this experience marked the spring as medicinally potent (and therefore morally "good") to those who could recognize its qualities.

While drinking from medicinal mineral springs laid the historic foundation for the territory's healthful status, taking the waters was merely one component of a series of holistic "acts of incorporation" that a visitor could undertake in the landscape. In *kurorti,* like Borjomi, climate therapies and "terrain cures" developed during the Soviet period encouraged a bodily porosity, a perviousness to place that was no longer thought possible in industrializing urban centers from which workers would travel.[14] The human body was to become a series of permeable membranes–the skin, the lungs, the gastric system, and certainly the mouth and tongue–through which restorative features of the landscape should pass. *Kurorti* were protected territories.

Extensive sanatoria complexes spatialized these acts of bodily incorporation. Health resorts manifested the universal "right to rest" enshrined into the Soviet constitution in 1936.[15] Certainly, visitors dined and slept there, but the sanatoria's primary function was to facilitate bodily engagement with the curative or invigorating properties latent in the region's specific air currents, plant compositions, solar aspect, and, of course, hydrogeologic formations. In addition to drinking a region's mineral waters, for example, visitors could undergo balneological treatments, bathing in them, or immerse themselves in healing muds (peloidotherapies).[16] Solaria and sunbathing terraces were oriented toward the south where nurses enforced timed rotations, using mirrors to concentrate sunlight on targeted zones of the skin.[17] Low alpine landscapes like those around Borjomi were particularly favored for the intensity of the solar radiation found there, preferred by patients suffering from lupus or eczema.

Sanatorium camps, comprised of temporary tent-like structures, were deployed for climate therapies, regulating exposure to open air that might fortify the naked body against colds and infectious diseases.[18] They could be repositioned across the sanatoria's grounds according to the changing breezes, as door flaps were opened

1 The Deepest Site – Juvenile Water Edition, "Borjomi – The Deepest Site," https://thedeepestsite.com/int_en/?country_code=int_en (accessed October 4, 2023).

2 Ibid.

3 Paul Manning, *The Semiotics of Drink and Drinking* (Continuum, 2012), 97.

4 Susanne Højlund, "Taste as a Social Sense: Rethinking Taste as a Cultural Activity," *Flavour* 4, no. 6 (2015): 2.

5 Maradia Tsaava, "Georgia Nationalises Iconic Mineral Water Due to Russian Sanctions," *Institute for War and Peace Reporting* (June 14, 2022), https://iwpr.net/global-voices/georgia-nationalises-iconic-mineral-water-due-russian-sanctions.

6 Civil.ge, "Georgian Govt Receives 7.73% of Borjomi Shares," *Civil Georgia* (June 14, 2023), https://civil.ge/archives/495813.

7 Borjomi, "Live Water, Georgian Legend," https://borjomi.com/en (accessed November 10, 2023).

8 Amy Trubek, *The Taste of Place, A Cultural Journey into Terroir* (University of California Press, 2008).

9 Højlund, "Taste as a Social Sense: Rethinking Taste as a Cultural Activity," 2.

10 Johanna Conterio, "Curative Nature: Medical Foundation of Soviet Nature Protection, 1917–1941," *Slavic Review* 78, no. 1 (2019).

11 Manning, *The Semiotics of Drink and Drinking*, 96.

Previous: Tsaghveri Spring efflorescence.

and closed to capture microclimates, ensuring the appropriate temperature and velocity for absorption through the skin and lungs.[19] A regime of walking on carefully graded pathways drew patients outward from the sanatorium into the broader landscape. Visitors could walk in prescribed intervals and various steepness levels, harnessing local topographies for their cardiac and respiratory benefits.[20]

The definitive guidebook to the Soviet health resorts in Georgia focuses on the description of the biophysical and climatological features of each landscape, as well as the sensory phenomena that visitors might experience in relation to them. These descriptions are mostly absent of any argument for why such experiences might be valuable, taking for granted the shared cultural meaning of such phenomena for the health of the human body. For instance, the entry for the village of Libani notes that "the air is absolutely clean, loaded with pine fragrance" including "spruce [*Picea orientalis*], pine [*Pinus kochiana*], and silver fir [*Abies nordmanniana*]."[21] Indeed, visitors sought low alpine landscapes like those surrounding Borjomi, specifically for the opportunity to breathe amidst evergreen forests, desirous of the fortifying "atmospheric vitamins" they emitted, which could be absorbed only through respiration.[22]

These place descriptions speak to a highly attuned, intimate apprehension of, and semiotic significance granted to, for example, the smell of a forest or the taste of spring water. They evidence a holistic, ecological relation to place, an uncommon and nuanced territorial literacy. These situated treatments were not merely consumed like a pill but felt, and sensed as they passed across the frontier of the body, affirming the presence of vital landscape matter derived from the precise conditions of the local landscape. Certainly, mineral waters were consumed with this understanding: more than a mere sum of nutritious ingredients, their taste signaled complex, interrelated landscape processes that collectively formulated a unique and necessarily situated therapeutic. Taken at the precise point of their emergence, individuals drinking the water made explicit connections between the source's context and its unique qualities, discernible through taste.

Following nearly a century and a half of landscape-based therapies, the health resorts in the Borjomi region were largely abandoned during the economic catastrophe of the Soviet Union's fall. Today, built vestiges of these "tasting activities"–the once-grand sanatoria, purpose-built railway, cultural halls, and libraries–stand in silence, eerily abandoned and crumbling after a generation of disuse. A handful of remnant structures harbor those displaced by the territorial wars of the 1990s and 2000s, a stopgap that has extended into decades. Villages that sprang up to house the *kurort's* cultural and service workers are now sparsely populated; young people have left in search of employment and education opportunities in Tbilisi or abroad.[23] Absent the Socialist "structures of desire" that linked ecological and human worlds, which evoked a communal taste for place, the territory's healthcare infrastructures and the landscape cures to which they once afforded access no longer cohere.[24]

Yet the flow of mineral waters persists through its basaltic mesas, materially linking actions on the surface. Though the Soviet project of a medicalized nature might be dismissed as purely instrumental, evidencing an appreciation not of "nature itself," but of what nature might offer the human body (and the body politic), shared cultural memory of the waters' meaning endures. Indeed, health landscapes in the Caucasus were valued not only as individual retreats for resting and healing, but consciously cultivated as public venues for social encounters and acculturation. Through shared aesthetic appreciation and sensory experiences in native landscapes, visitors and locals enacted social relations and developed common sensibilities with people across the Union.

For those who still reside in the historic *kurorti* on the plateaus above Borjomi, each village's spring source remains a convivial gathering place, a persistent site of commensality. Fountains that mark the point of their emergence are communally tended, swept, repaired, or improved, and often furnished with a bright aluminum cup placed into an inset niche. Those who recall their stays at Libani or Kechkhobi still pull to the side of the road to collect water to take with them.

Common Senses

In 2020, US media agency Battery launched a series of commercials introducing bottled Borjomi to the American market, whose revised packaging notably omits the renowned mineralization content label. In each ad, pairs of actors perform tasting the water for the first time, with reactions ranging from "that's pretty good," to "I'm going to pass." Though not to everyone's taste, apparently, the ad makes a point to tell us what its mineral flavors index: "Nature," it admonishes, "You just forgot what nature tastes like." Bottled and exported to consumers who have no link to the landscape from which it originates, IDS Borjomi finds it necessary to both explain the water's flavor to a Western audience (justifying that it has any at all) and provide compelling reasons for its consumption. As a "floating signifier," taken out of its local and regional context, Borjomi is tethered to a broad and morally tinged "naturalness," reducing the experience of the water's taste to an individual's preference and taste buds.

However, historical conceptions of this water closer to home demonstrate that senses of taste can encompass more than an individual's sensorial apparatus. As anthropologists Carole Counihan and Susanne Højlund suggest, our understanding of senses merely as passive receptors shaped by an outer (cultural) world should be broadened. Instead, they prompt an examination of how taste extends beyond private experience and "becomes accessible for others to engage in and possibly to share," actively shaping the social space between people and that which is sensed and consumed.[25] While the chemical composition of mineral waters remains fairly stable, fluctuating in a broad geologic timescale, cultivated public tastes are mobile and diffuse, transmitted through faster and more dynamic processes of human interaction, shifting political and institutional structures, and distribution practices.

In today's Borjomi, shifts in this matrix reveal a set of sensibilities in transition. During the summer, Tbilisians and Russian ex-pats might retreat to the villages on the plateaus above the town to take fresh air for a few weeks, renting rooms in private guest houses. Meanwhile, newer tourists to the region from beyond the former Soviet

republics usually only spend an afternoon or night in Borjomi, a convenient stopover between the capital and the Black Sea coast. Given a handful of hours, a visitor's primary task is to stroll through the old town toward Borjomi Central Park, passing through a peculiar mix of neo-Tudor pastiche hotels, halal restaurants, carnival games, and souvenir shops, while groups of young men purvey off-road forest adventure tours on mud-caked Polaris UTVs. Despite the built vestiges that evidence traditional modes of drinking and healing, new audiences bring diverse values and desires, and an emergent lack of consensus about the future of this landscape.

Without the stabilizing force of the All-Union project, glitches and slippages in semiotic processes become apparent. In the park, tourists can still partake of the original Ekaterina spring source in view of the historic bottling plant. An IDS Borjomi employee, sporting the company's branded polo, distributes small plastic cups filled with water from the fountain, replacing the nurse who once measured and dispensed it in doses. Even those familiar with the bottled product are startled by the intensity of this water's taste. Direct from the source, it lacks the additional carbonation infused into the product during packaging and refreshing crispness derived from refrigeration. Instead, it emerges from below the surface as it always has: warm, near the temperature of a human body, as a thick, sulfurous, and salty suspension, an artifact of an unseen realm. However, while the water persists, its audience increasingly lacks context and a framework for valuing such experiences. Those sensibilities–driving actions that connected landscape and body–reside precariously in memory and performance alone.

Given that designers' tools are limited primarily to what can be left behind in landscapes, gestures that are endlessly interpretable, we cannot reconstruct coherent and singular place meanings in the manner that continental empires have. Global markets ensure that the implications of sensory phenomena are up for grabs, and available to anyone who can claim them. In the absence of state and social institutions that define the value of engaging with places on hydrogeologic terms, for example, could landscape architects play a role in rechoreographing situated, sensory experiences for broad audiences? Historic modes of engaging landscapes–rituals of breathing air, walking relief, and drinking waters–might provide a template for recultivating shared tastes for specific landscape qualities, making them accessible to anyone with sensory capacities. Yet, rather than fostering consensus on sense meanings and attempting to close semantic loops, we might instead orchestrate embodied, sensory exchanges with place as a valued end in itself.

12 Nicola Perullo, *Taste as Experience: The Philosophy and Aesthetics of Food* (Columbia University Press, 2016).

13 M.K. Vadachkoria, G.A. Ushveridze & J.A. Jaliashvili, *Health Resorts of the Georgian SSR* (Sabchota Sakartvelo Publishers, 1987), 342.

14 Johanna Conterio Geisler, "The Soviet Sanatorium: Medicine, Nature, and Mass Culture in Sochi, 1917-1991" (dissertation, Harvard University, 2014).

15 Diane P. Koenker, *Club Red: Vacation Travel and the Soviet Dream* (Cornell University Press, 2013), 6.

16 Ibid, 78.

17 Conterio Geisler, "The Soviet Sanatorium," 112, 342–43.

18 Ibid., 335–36.

19 Ibid., 162–65, 201.

20 Frederick Forchheimer & Ernest Edward Irons, *Forchheimer's Therapeusis of Internal Disease*, Vol. 3 (D. Appleton Company, 1915), 646.

21 Vadachkoria, Ushveridze & Jaliashvili, *Health Resorts of the Georgian SSR*, 345.

22 Edward Poldosky, *Red Miracle: The Story of Soviet Medicine* (The Beechhurst Press, 1947), 190–94.

23 Maradia Tsaava, "Young Georgians Abandon Rural Life for the Capital," Institute for War and Peace Reporting (March 28, 2023), https://iwpr.net/global-voices/young-georgians-abandon-rural-life-capital.

24 Elizabeth Cullen Dunn, "Postsocialist Spores: Disease, Bodies, and the State in the Republic of Georgia," *American Ethnologist* 35, no. 2 (2008): 254.

25 Caroline Counihan & Susanne Højlund, *Making Taste Public: Ethnographies of Food and the Senses* (Bloomsbury Academic, 2018), 1.

Opposite: Tsaghveri Spring.

AI
HISANO
#4011
COLOR OF

CAPITALISM-TRAINED EYES AND THE VISUAL APPETITE

Ai Hisano is an associate professor at the Graduate School of Interdisciplinary Information Studies at the University of Tokyo. She specializes in the history of the senses, business history, and the history of technology with a particular focus on the 20th-century US. Her first book, *Visualizing Taste: How Business Changed the Look of What You Eat* (Harvard University Press, 2019), won the Hagley Prize in Business History and the Shimizu Hiroshi Award (Japanese Association for American Studies).

+ ADVERTISING, INFORMATION STUDIES

"How green are canned green beans? How yellow is butter, or salad oil, or mayonnaise? ...How white is white flour?"[1]

A food chemist working at the US Department of Agriculture (USDA) asked this question to the readers of the trade journal *Food Industries* in 1941. He continued to insist on the importance of accurate measurement and determination of a "correct" color for food to appeal to consumers' eyes. However, knowing and creating a "right" food color was not just about attracting consumers – it was even more important to make food look "natural," or to reproduce what consumers believe to be a natural color of food, for example, the "right" redness for tomatoes and orange shades for oranges. Another USDA chemist likewise noted in 1939 that "to gain this eye appeal the color of a given food must be normal and right."[2] His emphasis on the "normal and right" color of foods suggests that the sense of sight was not simply a personal sensation or perception; rather, the visual modality was a shared experience that could be normalized and standardized. These government scientists who specialized in food research not only encouraged, but also authorized food producers and retailers to attend to and control the color of foods.

Popular expectations about natural colors of food have become increasingly standardized since the last decades of the 19th century. With the rise of mass-production and mass-marketing strategies, the industrialization of agriculture, and the development of food-coloring technologies, uniformity and consistency became key components of agricultural producers' and food processors' efforts to create and market what they imagined to be the natural look of foods. Oranges became always more orange regardless of seasons or production sites; butter came to look uniformly yellow all year round; and the red shade of cherry-flavored soft drinks and strawberry cake icing came to look alike. Even homemade cakes could look identical when made with cake mixes and packaged frosting. Masses of standardized, clean, bright produce became a common feature of modern supermarkets to present "freshness" to customers.

The desire to standardize a color of nature was not limited to food. According to Elaine Ayers, color standardization as a concept had already existed among alchemists and artists in 15th-century Europe, and it eventually became a dream for naturalists to standardize botanical taxonomy in the 18th century.[3] Standardization of color was meant to communicate visual sensations that were supposedly different from person to person so that, for example, what naturalists found in the field could be brought back home and recorded for later reference. In the food industry, color standardization allowed agricultural growers and food manufacturers to reproduce the identical color of their product whenever it was made or whoever made it.

Standardization of color was a challenging process. Diverse agents, including government scientists, agricultural producers, food processors, chemical companies, and advertisers, invested enormous amounts of money and effort to create a color of food that many people would eventually take for granted as natural. This essay explores this complex, and colorful, history of creating standardized food colors by focusing on the United States from the late 19th to the early 20th century.

What Color Is Your Banana?

When banana imports to the US began in the 1840s, at least two varieties came from Central and South America (mainly Cuba and Panama): the Cuban Red with red-purplish skin and the yellow Gros Michel variety, which later became more common in the US.[4] Both red and yellow bananas appeared in various media intended primarily for middle- and upper-class consumers during the 1870s and 1880s.[5] For instance, an 1871 lithograph, *Fruits of the Tropics*, included both varieties, along with other "tropical" fruits. *Mrs. Lincoln's Boston Cook Book*, first published in 1884, introduced a recipe for "Tropical Snow," which called for six "red bananas" and other "tropical" foods, including oranges and coconut. The dessert was layers of orange and banana slices, sprinkled thickly with coconut and powdered sugar on top.[6] These examples suggest that many middle- and upper-class Americans knew about red bananas, or at least they could recognize the red variety.

After the 1890s, as the importation of bananas increased and their retail price declined, the fruit became a popular food item – *Scientific American* even called the banana the "poor man's fruit."[7] Per capita banana consumption rose from 18.1 pounds in 1915 to 23.4 pounds in 1928.[8] When bananas began to reach a broader population, fruit shipping companies, most notably the United Fruit Company, began planting and distributing only the yellow variety. Because the Gros Michel had thicker skin than red bananas, it was more suitable for shipping to distant markets than red varieties.[9] Although the red bananas continued to appear on the market sporadically, yellow became the dominant color American consumers saw at the market, and it eventually became what they expected as an indication of good, mature bananas.

As the import of yellow bananas increased, their images pervaded advertisements and cookbooks. In their recipe leaflets and advertisements, fruit shipping firms like United Fruit not only promoted the consumption of bananas but also explained how to tell bananas' ripeness based on their skin colors. They usually included a color image showing unripe bananas with a green tinge and fully ripe yellow bananas.[10] In so doing, food companies and advertisers provided consumers with "color education," teaching them how bananas should look.

"Natural, Bright, Fresh Meat Color"

The creation of a natural color of food also involved the physical management of food products. The careful treatment of animals, for example, was essential for meat packers to prevent "unnatural" colors. Meat color resulted from a complex mixture of factors, including the breed, age, and sex of animals, the type of feeding, the part of the meat, animals' physical conditions, and slaughtering operations.[11] Meat from older animals tended to be darker in color. When the flesh of an animal was overheated before slaughter, it often assumed a dark "fiery appearance" and frequently developed a sour odor after slaughtering.[12] A 1913 meat packing manual noted that "no animal should be killed after a long drive or rapid run about the pasture" and it was "always better in such cases to permit the animal to rest overnight rather than to risk spoiling the meat."[13] In the early 20th century, knocking or stunning cattle was the major means of slaughtering animals, but these methods tended to prevent free blood flow and caused discoloration of the flesh. Another packing manual, published in 1905, warned packers about the potential loss of profits due to "undue violence" such as striking animals across the back with heavy sticks or prodding them unnecessarily. Great care needed to be taken to promote the free flow of blood and to prevent the discoloration of meat, the author advised.[14]

Making a natural color for cured meat products, such as bacon, sausages, and hams, was also critical for the meat-packing business. It often used various additives that helped to brighten and stabilize the red color of the finished product. As the use of synthetic dyes became increasingly common in the food industry by the early 20th century, meat packers used them for cured meat products.[15] One Chicago chemical company advertised various preservatives and dyes for coloring sausages and hams in its 1901 meat packing manual: the company's dye "makes a NATURAL, BRIGHT, FRESH MEAT COLOR, and when used properly an expert *can not tell* that the color in sausage is artificial."[16] The advertisement suggested that artificial coloring was indispensable for producers to create the finished product's natural appearance.

1 Gordon W. McBride, "How to Tell What Color It Is," *Food Industries* 13, no. 9 (September 1941): 41.

2 B. I. Masurovsky, "How to Obtain the Right Food Color," *Food Industries* 11, no. 1 (January 1939): 13.

3 Elaine Ayers, "Coded Colours: Botanical Histories of Colour Standardization," *The Site Magazine* 40, no. 2 (2019), https://www.thesitemagazine.com/read/codedcolours.

4 Peter Chapman, *Bananas: How the United Fruit Company Shaped the World* (Canongate, 2007); Dan Koeppel, *Banana: The Fate of the Fruit That Changed the World* (Hudson Street Press, 2008); John Soluri, *Banana Cultures: Agriculture, Consumption, and Environmental Change in Honduras and the United States* (University of Texas Press, 2005).

5 In the mid-19th century, both red and yellow bananas were a luxury for most American consumers.

6 Mary Johnson Bailey Lincoln, *Mrs. Lincoln's Boston Cook Book: What to Do and What Not to Do in Cooking* (Roberts Brothers, 1884), 393.

7 Mel T. Cook, "The Banana," supplement, *Scientific American* (September 23, 1905): 24847.

8 Harvard University Graduate School of Business Administration, Exhibits Presented for the Harvard Advertising Awards, vol. 8, pt. 1, "Report and Recommendations on Filed Survey for the Fruit Dispatch Company," May 13, 1940, Ms. Div. SPGD H339a, Baker Library Historical Collections, Harvard Business School.

9 Chapman, *Bananas*, 19; Koeppel, *Banana*, xii, xiv; Soluri, *Banana Cultures*, 39.

10 Fruit Dispatch Company, "From the Tropics to Your Table: Eighty-Three Tested Banana Recipes," 1926, box 4, Product Cookbooks Collection (PCC), Archives Center, National Museum of American History, Smithsonian Institution, Washington, DC; Fruit Dispatch Company, "A Study of the Banana: Its Every-day Use and Food Value," 1942, box 4, PCC; Fruit Dispatch Company Advertisement, *Ladies' Home Journal* (March 1926).

11 "Here Are Facts on Color Changes," *The National Provisioner* 143, no. 27 (December 31, 1960): 10; Jerry Lee Mautz, "A Discussion of the History and Development of the In-Store Merchandising and Packaging of Fresh Red Meat with Emphasis on the Effect of Polyvinyl Chloride Film on a Traditional Cellophane Market" (masters' thesis, Michigan State University, 1966): 25–26; Gordon L. Robertson, *Food Packaging: Principles and Practice* (Marcel Dekker, 1993), 433.

12 B. Heller & Co., *Secrets of Meat Curing and Sausage Making: How to Cure Hams, Shoulders, Bacon, Corned Beef, Etc., and How to Make All Kinds of Sausage, Etc., and Comply with All Pure Food Laws* (B. Heller, 1913), 186.

13 Ibid.

14 F. W. Wilder, *The Modern Packing House* (Nickerson and Collins, 1905), 72–73.

15 McArthur, Wirth & Co., *Butchers' and Packers' Tools and Machinery* (McArthur, Wirth & Co., 1900), 74–76.

16 B. Heller Advertisement in *Butchers' and Packers' Tools*, 78. Emphasis in the original.

Another additive that meat packers commonly used was sweeteners like glucose and corn syrup. According to the USDA's 1921 report, bacon cured with granulated cane sugar turned the ideal color of golden yellow when fried; whereas bacon cured with corn sugar tended to turn light- or dark-brown.[17]

The relationships between the color of meat and product quality were by no means natural, however. Rather, the idea that a bright red shade was an indication of good quality meat was historically and culturally constituted. Traditionally, words such as *bright* and *cherry red* were used to describe the preferred color of meat, particularly beef, and *white* and *creamy white* for beef fat.[18] For example, a food purchasing manual for housewives, published in 1934, asserted that the color of good beef was "bright cherry red and the flesh firm and fine grained, well mottled with a creamy-white fat and having a good outer covering of brittle, flaky, white fat."[19] The yellow color of fat and tissues could be a sign of disease.[20] The fat of aged animals also assumed a yellowish color; hence the meat was usually tougher than younger cows.[21] Yet in many cases, the color of fat varied from white to straw color and yellow, depending on the kinds of cattle feed: when cows were fed primarily on corn or grass, fat assumed a deep-yellow color. Moreover, the color of meat did not always indicate eating quality: meat color turned to gray or brown with little change in taste, though grayish and brown shades could suggest bacterial infection. Producers' and consumers' expectations about a natural color of meat encouraged meat packers to control and create the "fresh" and natural red color, which in turn reinforced the popular perception about food color.

Visualizing Color Expectations

Popular expectations about a color of food became increasingly standardized due to the introduction of color printing and new marketing strategies. Cookbooks and women's magazines had long been teaching housewives how to choose foods based on color.[22] An 1823 cookbook advised readers that a salmon should be "of fine red, [the gills particularly,] the scales bright," and there should be "a whiteness between flakes."[23] In 1893, an article in the *Ladies' Home Journal* noted that high-quality beef was "clear red in color; a pink hue signifie[d] the presence of disease, while that of a dark purple indicate[d] that death resulted from natural causes."[24] Chromatic information in these 19th-century recipes was based primarily on written texts, printed in black and white. Because there were no visual references in these recipes, what a "clear red" color for meat meant depended largely on consumers' experience and local market conditions.

During the 1920s and 1930s, the growth of national magazines, the expansion of national advertisements, and the increasing use of color printing provided consumers not only with eye-appealing illustrations but also with standardized visual references that they would recognize as the natural and "right" color of certain food products. As colorful food advertisements increasingly appeared in national magazines, a growing number of consumers across the country saw the same image wherever they lived. Women in New York City, Chicago, and San Francisco saw the same advertisements for Sunkist oranges and Swift's Premium ham featured in the *Ladies' Home Journal, Good Housekeeping*, and other mass-circulated magazines. Nationally distributed color printing helped to teach consumers the idealized and standardized image of the right, natural color of various food products.

As the use of color printing rapidly grew among food manufacturers in the first decades of the 20th century, advertising agents, printing firms, and manufacturers of various goods generally had come to believe that color was more effective than black-and-white advertisements, particularly for attracting female consumers. Advertisers believed that women were more susceptible to colors, so that the extra cost for four-color printing would be worth spending to appeal to "feminine interest."[25] In the mid- to late-1920s, many women's magazines increasingly featured four-color printing, which presented more vivid images and "faithful pictorial effects" than two-color images.[26]

As food was one of the products that was believed to be purchased predominantly by women, food companies were among the principal users of color in their promotion materials, believing that color would "whet the appetite."[27] As more advertisers turned to color images and as popular magazines began reducing their prices for color pages, colorful images of foods increasingly appeared in advertisements, giveaway cookbooks, and popular magazines. These colorful illustrations served to represent, disseminate, and reinforce cultural expectations about the color of foods.

Standards for Natural Color

If color printing offered consumers standardized visual references, grade standards provided agricultural producers and food manufacturers with an "objective" way of measuring and understanding product quality while reinforcing the real or perceived connections between color and food (its eating quality in particular). Grade standards for fruits and vegetables provided a shared definition of how agricultural products should look. Along with size and shape, color was an important criterion used for grading almost all produce. Grading systems, established by federal and state governments, helped to standardize not only the color of foods traded on the market but also what producers, merchants, and consumers expected to be the natural and "good" color of foods by categorizing fruits and vegetables into grades such as "fancy," "choice," and "U.S. No. 1."

Since the late 19th century, agricultural cooperative leaders had advocated the importance of grading fruits and vegetables to supply uniform and high-quality produce.[28] However, it was not until the 1910s that federal and state governments began establishing grade standards. One of the earliest standards was Maine's quality standard for apples, issued in 1910. By 1917, most of the fruit-producing states had enacted grade standard laws that specified the color, size, and shape of foods that could be marketed under specific grades.[29] For instance, under California's 1917 Fresh Fruit, Nut, and Vegetable Standardization Act, oranges needed to attain at least 25 percent yellow or orange color before picking.[30] The USDA established the first federal standard in 1917 for grading potatoes, followed by other fruits and vegetables.[31] These government grade standards helped in the marketing of farm products by providing a common language for wholesale trading.

These grade standards determined the market price. Market buyers usually paid 40 to 50 cents per box more for better-colored oranges than for fruits with green tinges or light orange shades.[32] Fruit shippers and traders believed that consumers would pay more for brighter fruits. For instance, on November 23, 1909, the price of "well colored" Florida oranges was $2 per box in the New York market, while "green and poor" fruit was sold at $1.25 per box.[33] Higher prices not only reflected the popular perception of acceptable color, but also helped to educate consumers that brighter oranges were "better" quality.

Quantifying Color

To establish standards and hence create standardized natural colors of food, producers sought to measure and quantify color. Among the most basic ways was to use color charts. Food producers and researchers compared the colors of their finished products to the standard shown on the chart to determine whether the finished product attained the "right" color. One of the color systems that was widely used (and is still used today) in the food industry was the Munsell system, originated by Albert H. Munsell, a professor of drawing at the Massachusetts Normal Art School in Boston, in 1905.[34] Munsell created what he called an "Atlas," comprising color charts

17 Ralph Hoagland, "Substitutes for Sucrose in Curing Meats," *USDA Bulletin* no. 928 (January 7, 1921): 22.

18 M. A. Price, "Development of Carcass Grading and Classification Systems," in S. D. Morgan Jones (ed.), *Quality and Grading of Carcasses of Meat Animals* (CRC Press, 1995), 188.

19 Alexander Todoroff, *Food Buying Today* (Grocery Trade Publishing House, 1934), 83. See also Armour & Company, Department of Home Economics, "Meat Selection, Preparation and Many Ways to Serve," 1934, Hagley Museum and Library, Wilmington, DE; "Meat Grades at Your Service," *Consumers' Guide* 4, no. 15 (October 18, 1937): 19.

20 Thomas Walley, *A Practical Guide to Meat Inspection* (William R. Jenkins, 1895), 14, 33.

21 H. W. Norton, "Meat Demonstration," *Sixteenth Annual Report of the Pennsylvania Department of Agriculture* (1910), 530.

22 See Lincoln, *Mrs. Lincoln's Boston Cook Book*; Maria Parloa, *Miss Parloa's New Cookbook: A Guide to Marketing and Cooking* (C. T. Dillingham, 1880).

23 Maria Eliza Ketelby Rundell, *American Domestic Cookery Formed on Principles of Economy for the Use of Private Families* (Evert Duyckinck, 1823), 29.

24 Mary Lee White, "Selection of Meat and Poultry," *Ladies' Home Journal* (April 1893): 30. See also Fannie Merritt Farmer, "A Lesson on Marketing," *Boston Cooking School Magazine of Culinary Science and Domestic Economics* (December 1897): 204.

25 "Food Advertisers Aid American Art," *Printers' Ink Monthly* 14, no. 4 (April 1927): 54. See also Patricia Johnston, *Real Fantasies: Edward Steichen's Advertising Photography* (University of California Press, 1997), 242.

26 Guy Richards, "Shall We Use Color?" *Printers' Ink Monthly* 13, no. 1 (July 1926): 98. See also "Use of Four Color Advertising Continues to Increase," *J. Walter Thompson Company (JWT) Newsletter* no. 108, November 27, 1925, box MN7, JWT, Newsletter Collection, David M. Rubenstein Rare Book & Manuscript Library, Duke University, Durham, NC; Richard A. Dunne, "What Is the Trend in the Use of Color," *JWT Newsletter* no. 123, July 1925, box MN5, JWT, Newsletter Collection.

27 W. Livingston Larned, "The New Spirit in Color Advertising," *Printers' Ink Monthly* 6, no. 6 (June 1923): 132–34. See also Hester Conklin & Pauline Partridge, "Selling Appetites through the Consumer Magazines," *Advertising and Selling* 30, no. 7 (July 17, 1920): 12; "Food Advertisers Aid American Art," *Printers' Ink Monthly* 14, no. 4 (April 1927): 54; "Color in Newspaper Advertising," *Printers' Ink Monthly* 28, no. 2 (February 1934): 62.

28 B. F. Walton, "Grading and Packing Fruit to Meet the Wants of the Trade," *Pacific Rural Press* (June 8, 1895).

29 Steven Stoll, *The Fruits of Natural Advantage: Making the Industrial Countryside in California* (University of California Press, 1998), 90. See also W. S. Killingsworth, "Standardization Promotes Fruit Industry," *Pacific Rural Press* (February 1920), http://cdnc.ucr.edu/cgi-bin/cdnc?a=d&d=PRP19200214.2.60 (accessed Oct. 26, 2023).

Dainty Apricot
BEHR® P220-4

Fresh Artichoke
BEHR® M340-5

Mango Tango
BEHR® P240-4

Cauliflower
BEHR® M340-1

Cheerful Tangerine
BEHR® P210-5

Cyber Grape
BEHR® M570-4

So Blue-Berry
BEHR® S540-1

Watermelon Slice
BEHR® P180-5

Garden Cucumber
BEHR® M400-7

Classy Plum
BEHR® N570-4

Bold Avocado
BEHR® M360-6

Raspberry Crush
BEHR® M120-7

that arranged different colors in order. Each color (or hue) was arranged based on the scale of value (the lightness or darkness of a color) and chroma (the saturation or brilliance of a color).[35]

The Munsell color charts have become an important and convenient tool to create uniform color not only in the food industry but also in many other businesses and professions, including geology and botany. These systematically organized visual references helped to standardize, and hence *decontextualize*, sensory experience. In one sense, the discovery and distribution of new plants, including edible ones, were partly a product of colonial expeditions and imperial expansions. However, as Ayers points out, "each seemingly innocuous numbered" color ended up "obscuring the racial, gendered, and economic histories involved in their making."[36] The color chart, in other words, extracted the chromatic information from a material object embedded in a historical context. In another sense, standardization of color takes context away from individual experience. Suppose you are holding an apple or your favorite candies–how these foods look, as well as taste, may change depending on the context, including the surrounding conditions, mood, or memory associated with the food. Nevertheless, when color scientists examine food based on color charts and specify its color by a code or number, the actual eating experience and memory associated with it may not be a significant part of the visual modality. In this regard, while creating standardized visual references and color nomenclature, the color charts helped to normalize a new way of understanding bodily sensations. Rather than context-specific experience, senses came to be understood as biological (hence "objective") phenomena that could be investigated and understood in a laboratory.

The color charts were not the perfect solution for color standardization, however. Judging color with human eyes did not always provide uniform or consistent results, since it depended on the physical and psychological conditions of the viewer, such as lighting, the presentation of the sample, and the observer's fatigue.[37] Since no two persons responded to a given light or color stimulus in quite the same way, there were discrepancies in research data among researchers. Accordingly, color scientists began experimenting with new equipment called spectrophotometers to replace human eyes for color investigation in the 1920s and 1930s. Spectrophotometers provided quantitative measurements of larger color ranges than colorimeters by calculating the intensity of light reflected from a sample of foods and beverages.[38] It was not until the mid- to late-20th century that colorimeters and spectrophotometers became fully automatic. Yet these color-measurement instruments of the 1920s and 1930s allowed researchers to detect the color more uniformly and consistently than earlier equipment.

Color charts and measuring equipment provided scientists and food producers with "objective" knowledge about colors and a means for quantifying and standardizing the naturalness of food colors. As Jonathan Crary has shown in his study of the transformation of visual environments in 19th-century Europe, new ways of measuring and seeing colors in the early 20th century were a technological imperative for "capitalist modernization" to "recode the activity of the eye, to regiment it, to heighten its productivity and to prevent its distraction."[39] Color, like sight in general, was no longer a personal sensation–even human eyes were replaced by equipment. The apparatus for color analysis altered how people understood colors fundamentally, and the rationalized and standardized perception of color became essential for food producers to give foods a natural color consistently.

Conclusion

Today, most of us cannot escape from uniformly colored, bright foods, carefully engineered by producers and retailers, in almost any aisle of a grocery store – a bag of apples, a box of breakfast cereal, and a tub of margarine invariably offer a uniform color, as well as flavor and taste. Not only has the color of food become more uniform than before, but the variety of food available on the market has also become standardized, as shown by the yellow banana example.

This creation of standardized colors in the foodscape was a distinctive historical construction, along with the rise of new political and economic powers starting in the late 19th century. Climate and other environmental conditions determined the quality of agricultural produce harvested in certain regions, affecting how growers controlled the colors of their products. Partly due to global and domestic market competition and available technologies, agricultural producers and traders promoted specific varieties and shades of produce, which many consumers eventually considered their natural colors. Scientists and food processors sought to quantify visual sensations and to attain "objective" knowledge about the right and natural color of a certain food. Federal and state governments employed regulatory powers to define how food should look on the market by establishing food grading systems and setting color standards for certain products. Colorful advertisements, recipe leaflets, and popular magazines provided consumers with powerful visual references, presenting ideas about the natural color of foods. Shifting consumer conceptions about the safety, naturalness, and wholesomeness of foods also had a substantial impact on manufacturers' business decisions on food color control. Popular perception of natural foods and producers' efforts to create natural colors to increase their profits created *naturalness* as a complex characteristic of foods.

The rise of consumer capitalism came with fundamental changes in the look and appearance of the material world. This new visuality was more uniformly colorful than in the past as the senses became a product of mass production, standardization, and rationalization. This management of sight in the food industry epitomizes the mobilization of the senses in the capitalist system. The upshot was that color standardization engendered not only the creation of a uniform look but also a fundamental change in the understanding and conceptualization of sensory experience: one's sensation was no longer a personal, subjective, or intimate corporeal experience but rather something to be investigated scientifically, mass produced, and controlled. Over time, business has created an entirely new sensory world.

30 James H. Deering, *Supplement to the Codes and General Laws of the State of California of 1915, Showing the Changes Affecting the Codes and the General Laws for the Years 1917 and 1919* (Bancroft-Whitney, 1919), 1078.

31 Following potato standards, the federal government established standards for other vegetables, fruits, and nuts in 1917; butter, cheddar cheese, nonfat dry milk, and certain other dairy products in 1919; rice, dry beans, peas and related products in 1924; eggs in 1925; poultry in 1930; beef, veal and calf, and lamb and mutton carcasses in 1926; and canned, frozen, and dried fruits and vegetables, and other related products such as preserves in 1928. H. E. Erdman, *American Produce Markets* (D. C. Heath, 1928), 255; Stoll, *The Fruits of Natural Advantage*, 90; Bureau of Agricultural Economics, USDA, "Handbook of United States Standards for Grading and Marketing Fresh Fruits and Vegetables," Miscellaneous Publication No. 190 (June 1934): 3–4.

32 L. P. Kirkland, "The 'Color Added' Situation," *Proceedings of the Florida State Horticultural Society* 49 (1936): 105.

33 "Market Reports," *Ocala Evening Star* (November 23, 1909).

34 Hunt & Pointer, *Measuring Color*, 159.

35 Dorothy Nickerson, "History of the Munsell Color System," *Color Engineering* 7, no. 5 (September–October 1969); Yeshajahu Pomeranz & Clifton E. Meloan, *Food Analysis: Theory and Practice*, 3rd ed. (Aspen, 1994), 92–93. For the development of the Munsell Color system, see Regina Lee Blaszczyk, *The Color Revolution* (MIT Press, 2012), 45–70.

36 Ayers, "Coded Colours."

37 See D. B. Judd, "Precision of Color Temperature Measurements under Various Observing Conditions: A New Color Comparator for Incandescent Lamps," *Bureau of Standards Journal of Research* 5, no. 5 (November 1930): 11161–77; Dorothy Nickerson, "Application of Color Measurement in the Grading of Agricultural Products," USDA, Bureau of Agricultural Economics (January 1932).

38 See Kenneth A. Evelyn, "A Stabilized Photoelectric Colorimeter with Light Filters," *Journal of Biological Chemistry* 115, no. 1 (August 1936): 63–75; C. E. K. Mess, "The Measurement of Color," *JIEC* 13, no. 8 (August 1921): 729; R. B. Withrow, C. L. Shrewsbury & H. R. Kraybill, "The Design of a Precision Photoelectric Colorimeter," Analytical Edition, *Journal of Industrial and Engineering Chemistry* 8, no. 3 (May 1936): 214–19.

39 Jonathan Crary, *Techniques of the Observer: On Vision and Modernity in the Nineteenth Century* (MIT Press, 1992), 24.

THE
QUEEN
ROYAL
PRINCESS MAY

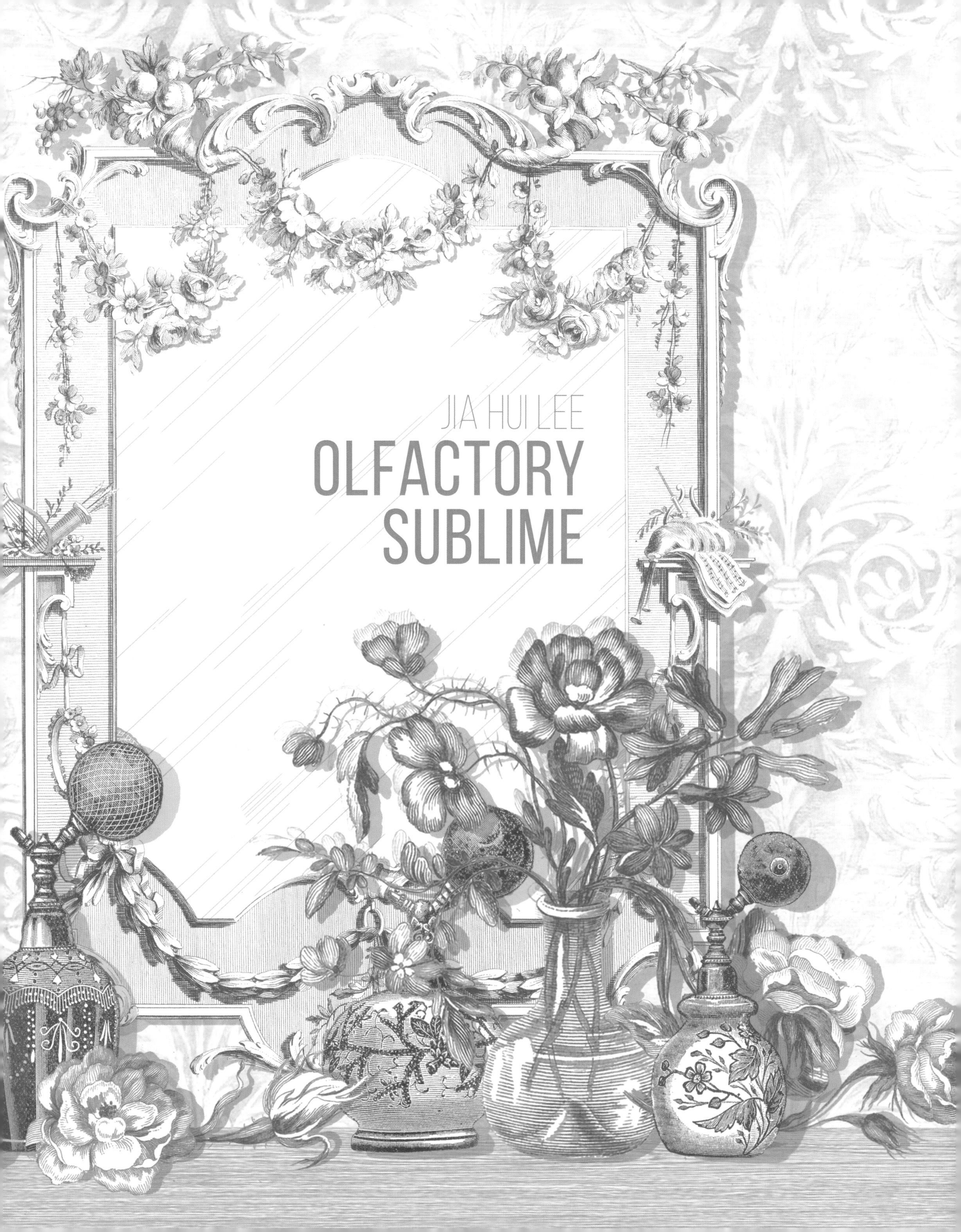

JIA HUI LEE

OLFACTORY SUBLIME

Jia Hui Lee is the Junior Professor of Science & Technology Studies at the University of Bayreuth and was the 2021–2023 Andrew W. Mellon Post-Doctoral Fellow in the John B. Hurford '60 Center for the Arts and Humanities at Haverford College, PA. He is an anthropologist of science and technology. His current research is a historically informed ethnography of various human-rodent encounters in Tanzania's zoological research, animal training, and pest management schemes.

+ ANTHROPOLOGY, SCIENCE + TECHNOLOGY STUDIES

We arrived at a large peach-colored function room of a retirement home to lead a "médiation," or outreach workshop, on odors. I was there to learn from Grégoire who works in the public engagement team at the International Museum of Perfumery in Grasse, a hillside town in southern France. My job that day was to help distribute *mouillettes*–little paper tabs that have been sprayed with fragrances–to the older men, women, and their caregivers who had gathered. Many residents at the home have dementia, Alzheimer's, and other aging-related conditions.

At first, no one spoke, and there was a stillness in the air. That is, until the workshop began. Grégoire promised that the scents he was about to share were one of the most powerful ways to recover memories, to remember.[1] Without ever naming a scent, he sprayed various chemicals onto a flutter of *mouillettes*. As I distributed the paper fingers, he invited the room to wave them like lace and breathe in their perfumes. Chatter, sometimes giggles, or sighs broke out suddenly around the room. Each time, Grégoire invited the participants to share memories that had come flooding back. Several people shared excitedly that the scents reminded them of the flower market on Place Aux Aires, another the fields of violets in Tourettes-sur-Loup. Madame Hubert said that it made her think of the day that Edith Piaf died in nearby Plascassier. Monsieur Nicolás, wielding a walking stick, announced in his Provençal dialect that the scent recalled a field of lavender, where he once "shagged a woman." "I ended up smelling like soap the whole week," he said to a room filled with laughter. By the end, the group had broken into song about flowers, love, and the countryside. As a spontaneous choral rendition of Luis Mariano's "L'amour est un bouquet de violettes" filled the room, Grégoire packed up the odor flasks and winked, saying, "These are magical potions."[2]

There was always something magical or supernatural about odors and the ability to smell them. Authors have written about the connection between smells and their imperceptible powers to seduce, attract, infect, and transcend.[3] Famously, the Latin root for the word perfume is *per fumus*, a word that effuses the conveying of prayer–by smoke–to the divine. In 2015, I spent several weeks working as an intern at the perfumery museum in Grasse to learn more about smell's magical qualities. I helped with exhibition catalogs, led a few guided visits, and explored the archives, which contained perfume composition guides, notes on chemical experiments, olfactory research, and a large collection of full and empty perfume bottles, some containing the original blend of a famous fragrance, such as Jicky (1889), one of the first made using synthetic compounds. At the museum, I became familiar with the Jean Carles Method–developed in the early 20th century–which trained me to remember and recognize many types of materials based on their similar or different odors. Years later, I would occasionally practice my training by identifying scents found in a friend's moisturizer. The reaction was not that different from having performed a magic trick, and soon I was often called upon at parties to sniff different tubes of cream that emerged from purses, dashboards, and drawers.

Today, the imperceptible power of odors continues to perplex. Among chemists, neuroscientists, and, increasingly, computer scientists, how people smell remains quite a mystery.[4] Researchers have proposed and challenged several hypotheses to explain olfaction: is it due to the structure of an odor molecule? Or its combinatorial effect on receptors? Are there proteins that transform odorous molecules so that they can attach to an olfactory neuron? Or could it be quantum osmic frequencies?[5] No surprises then that books about the sciences of smelling contain terms such as "secret" and "mystery."[6] These book titles are suffused with an element of augury–the skilled sensing of invisible signs–that lend olfaction its magical quality.

Much current scientific research around olfaction is driven by the possibility of detecting the meaning behind odors. Do they reveal hidden structures? Are they signs of certain phenomena? Understanding the hidden meanings conveyed by odors has been a long-time effort. Charles H. Piesse, a 19th-century chemist and purveyor of "exquisite new perfumes" concocted in his London laboratory, described the senses as sentinels whose cultivation offers "natural protection against various dangers."[7] As omens, odors foretell ominous, hidden threats. Citing an 1885 issue of the medical journal *Lancet*, Piesse argued that smell "seems to be the best indicator of goodness or badness, agreeable odours being as a rule quite harmless."[8] Over time, various hypotheses have posited that the structure of chemical compounds may signal certain sensory reactions, with each structure having a corresponding effect on olfactory receptors that register as specific odors in the brain. Manipulating these chemical structures, it is hoped, can change human behavior or transform urban environments. In Piesse's time, this meant changing the built environment to manipulate the physical flows of noxious odors. Sewers were buried underground, and slaughterhouses were relocated outside the city's limits.

Since Piesse's time, chemists have determinedly hoped that the molecular structure of organic compounds, such as its stereochemical configuration, polarity, and molecular weight, may determine an odor's qualities. For example, aromatics, a classification used for chemical structures that contain one or more rings of six carbons was thought to smell sweet and spicy. Although organic chemistry no longer classifies compounds by their smell, researchers are still trying to find a link between odorous experiences and molecular shape or structure. Understanding this link offers the possibility of being able to manipulate sensory experiences. If one can change the shape of molecules, one can shape the experience of smells and the behaviors prompted by them.[9]

Historians of technology have referred to the feelings of awe and amazement engendered through magnificent feats of engineering as the "technological sublime."[10] Large-scale engineering projects such as the Golden Gate Bridge in San Francisco connected lands separated by oceans. Others, like the Hoover Dam, generated power by flooding valleys. They inspired a sense of benign human dominion over the environment, a physical restructuring of a messy natural world to harness energy and compress space and time.[11] If in the 19th century, waterways were reengineered to hide their smells, then in the 21st, perfumers and chemists are trying to engineer odorant molecules.[12] As technologies and techniques of chemical analyses develop over time, which offer new ways for understanding *and* controlling how humans smell, could there perhaps be an olfactory sublime, a feeling of being awe-struck by engineered smells that affect, anticipate, and, even, heal? Could the desire to detect and identify invisible vapors, traces, and plasms be a search for exact and awe-inspiring methods of odor manufacture and manipulation?

Smelling What You Can't See

Leaving behind the Mediterranean foothills of the Alpes-Maritimes, I traveled to Tanzania in search of an answer. There, I spent eighteen months from 2017–2019 researching human and rodent relations. In particular, I was interested in learning from a group of people who train giant pouched rats (*Cricetomys ansorgei*) to detect landmines and tuberculosis by seeking out the odors that degrading explosives and infectious

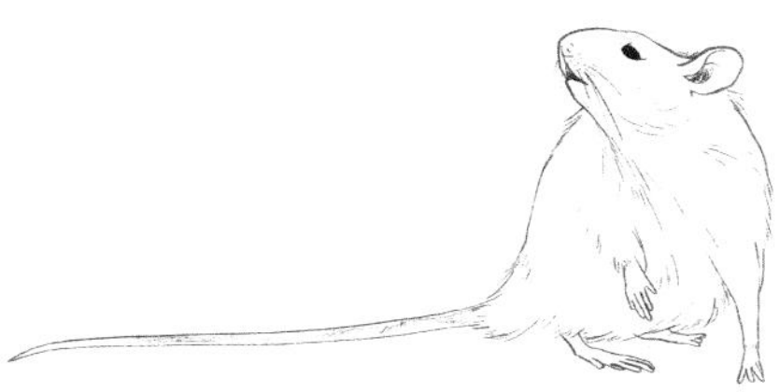

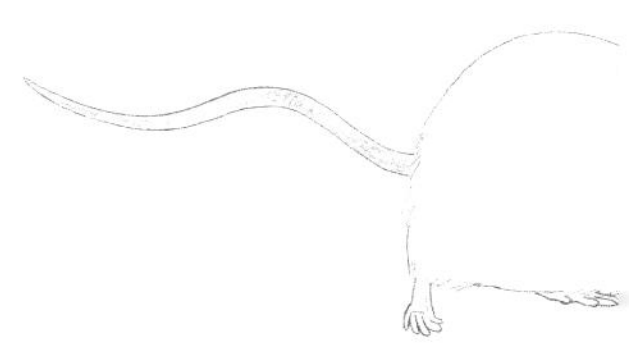

bacteria emit. Olfaction is the main sensory modality in rodents.[13] Smelling is key in shaping how rodents parent, socialize, learn, explore, forage food, and survive. Rodents have been shown to track odors to find their way to food or away from predators.[14] Rodents can even develop a preference for a new type of food after smelling its odor on the breath of another.[15] When mice are trained to discriminate specific odors from others, they can do so even when background odors are unfamiliar.[16]

Apopo, a humanitarian project in Morogoro, seeks to exploit this impressive olfactory ability in rats by training them to identify odors issuing from degrading explosives and TB-positive sputum [a mixture of saliva and mucus usually coughed up from the lower respiratory tract]. One easy way to do this is to pair food rewards with these target odors. Each time a young rat is given a target odor to sniff, it is also rewarded with food. As the training progresses, the rat then must pick out [or discriminate] target odors from a larger group. In the tuberculosis detection project, trained rats must show that they can correctly find the one, two, or three TB+ sputum samples out of a line of ten before they are certified to work on actual samples provided by various clinics and hospitals.

"What witchcraft [*uchawi*] is this?" one of the rat trainers recalled saying when she first encountered the project. She had been amazed by what she saw at the annual agricultural fair, where rodent trainers demonstrated to a curious public how they trained rats to detect TB. "When I saw this surprising thing, I wanted to learn how to do it," she explained, launching her on a career to become a rat trainer. "When I first heard about the rats from my cousin, I thought he was crazy," Ally, another trainer, told me in an interview. "Then I saw my cousin work with the rat, and the rat found TB infections so quickly. I wanted to know; how did they teach the rats?" The shock or surprise expressed by these rat trainers were echoed by many others who encountered the trained rats for the first time.

Even more experienced trainers admit that they never ceased to be impressed by the rats' abilities. One of the things that sometimes happens, they explained, is a rat signaling that a negative control sample–which had been confirmed negative often using smear microscopy–should have been positive for TB. "When we go and check with the patient who gave us this negative sample, we found that they were now TB+." This puzzled the trainers and the occasional epidemiologist or psychologist who visited the project. These rats could now

1 All names, apart from those of public figures, have been changed to pseudonyms.

2 Interestingly, there is an ongoing clinical trial to determine whether olfactory training would be "effective in protecting the memory and brain regions of people who are already showing signs of memory loss" [Development and Evaluation of Computerized Olfactory Training Program for Cognitive Decline in Early Alzheimer's Disease, 2021].

3 Constance Classen, David Howes & Anthony Synnott [eds], *Aroma: The Cultural History of Smell* [Routledge, 1994].

4 Veronique Greenwood, "O.K., Computer, Tell Me What This Smells Like," *New Yorker* [October 9, 2017], https://www.newyorker.com/tech/annals-of-technology/ok-computer-tell-me-what-this-smells-like.

5 Christina Agapakis, "Osmic Frequencies." *The New Inquiry* [February 13, 2015], https://thenewinquiry.com/osmic-frequencies/.

6 Luca Turin, *The Secret of Scent: Adventures in Perfume and the Science of Smell* [Ecco, 2006]; Chandler Burr, *The Emperor of Scent: A Story of Perfume, Obsession, and the Last Mystery of the Senses* [Random House, 2002].

7 Charles H. Piesse, *Olfactics and the Physical Senses* [Piesse and Lubin, 1887], 9.

8 Ibid., 87–88.

9 Catherine Bouvet, *Manipulations olfactives: enquête sur ces odeurs qui séduisent, guérissent, trahissent* [Payot, 2013].

10 David E. Nye, *American Technological Sublime* [MIT Press, 1994].

11 Ibid.; see also Leo Marx, *The Machine in the Garden: Technology and the Pastoral Ideal in America* [Oxford University Press, 2000].

12 Alain Corbin, *The Foul and the Fragrant: Odor and the French Social Imagination* [Harvard University Press, 1986].

13 Adil Ghani Khan, Manaswini Sarangi & Upinder Singh Bhalla, "Rats Track Odour Trails Accurately Using a Multi-Layered Strategy with Near-Optimal Sampling," *Nature Communications* 3, no. 1 [February 28, 2012]: 703, https://doi.org/10.1038/ncomms1712.

14 Alina Cristina Marin, Andreas T. Schaefer & Tobias Ackels, "Spatial Information from the Odour Environment in Mammalian Olfaction," *Cell and Tissue Research* 383, no. 1 [2021]: 473–83, https://doi.org/10.1007/s00441-020-03395-3.

15 Bennett G. Galef & Stephen W. Wigmore, "Transfer of Information Concerning Distant Foods: A Laboratory Investigation of the 'Information-Centre' Hypothesis," *Animal Behaviour* 31, no. 3 [1983]: 748–58, https://doi.org/10.1016/S0003-3472[83]80232-2.

augur a coming illness. Their ability could be life-changing for humans. Informing a person who has TB is important to ensure that they get access to treatment and to stop the person from transmitting the infection to others. A person's sputum infected with pulmonary TB contains scores of tiny, red-stained rods, each a TB bacterium, when seen under a light microscope. Counting the number of red-stained rods in a specific field of vision provides an estimate of the disease's progress. A negative sputum sample usually does not have any rods, or it has too few of them. Yet, some of these negative samples were presumably releasing odors that, for the trained rat, resembled those from sputum infected by TB. What were the rats smelling that no person could see through the microscope?

An Ancestry of Witches

In one of the attempts to understand rats' prescience for TB infection, the project staff invited Joy Milne of Perth, Scotland to see if her olfactory abilities could solve the conundrum. Joy Milne became famous for her ability to detect disease based on a person's smell. Her story has been recounted many times, even drawing the attention of scientists who designed experiments to test her capabilities. As the story goes, Milne had one day recognized a change in the odor of her husband. After pestering him to shower constantly, the odor persisted and Milne had to learn to ignore it. Almost ten years later, her husband was diagnosed with Parkinson's disease. When she attended a support group for people with Parkinson's, she was hit with the same odor.[17] Mixed in with an individual's own smell, she could unmistakably detect a specific, underlying odor common to all of the attendees. Could Parkinson's have a smell? And could knowing it help people spot early signs of the disease?

Follow up studies of Milne's incredible ability provided evidence that indeed Parkinson's did have a smell, and that Milne was able to detect it.[18] This was no surprise to those in Tanzania who work with TB-detecting rats. "Of course, many diseases have a smell. The question is who can smell it," Ally commented. He was discussing Milne's visit to the project. "I think we are all born with this talent," he went on, "but not all of us have trained to use it." And training was what Milne had to first do when she was given sputum samples to smell. These samples had been denatured so that the TB bacteria in them, if present, were neither active nor infectious. Milne was first given negative samples to smell, followed by positive ones. She took notes about their different qualities. Milne then selected different samples to smell again, noting how they differed from or resembled one another. Once Milne had trained herself on these odors, just as a rat would, she was then given unlabeled samples. She did almost as well as a trained rat in identifying TB+ samples.

Milne described the smell of the positive samples as being salty with a tinge of wet socks. She could also smell the breath of the person from whom the sputum came. What was striking was the way she could distinguish between the smells of the various TB positive sputum samples. Usually, TB positive sputum samples were categorized according to how many red-stained rods were visible in certain fields of vision under a microscope, from AFB 1+ to 3+, with AFB 3+ being the highest. AFB 3+ samples smelled a little like death, she said, with very little trace of the human's breath left. The three different categories also smelled distinctly different from one another, although with a common underlying quality of salty, wet socks. What Milne's experience suggests is that the rats were perhaps smelling the odorous result of an interaction between TB bacteria and human tissue, rather than just smelling the volatile organic compounds released by the bacteria. This could explain why some rats were able to augur a future diagnosis. They were smelling human tissue that had already been attacked by small, unnoticeable amounts of bacteria.

When I spoke with Milne later, I asked her about how people had reacted when they found out about her powerful ability, "Do they ask you to diagnose them? Would you tell?" Milne shook her head, "I do not tell people what I smell on them. I keep it to myself." When I asked why, she suggested that it could get her into trouble. "This ability is passed down through the women in my family," she explained. A relative of Milne's, too, has a way with her nose. "Who knows?" she pondered, "The witch burnings in Scotland [in the 17th century] probably targeted people like me."

Olfactory Sublime

Whether it was perfume, the recollection of memory, or tuberculosis diagnosis, olfaction–increasingly at the molecular level–offers tantalizing potentials for improving human life. The gambit lay in finding a way to analyze and manipulate odors at the molecular level. This is the argument made by Jérôme Golebiowski, whose laboratory I visited in 2015 at Université Nice Sophia Antipolis. His research is focused on achieving an intricate understanding of how olfaction works, usually by modeling the interactions of odorants, odorant binding proteins,

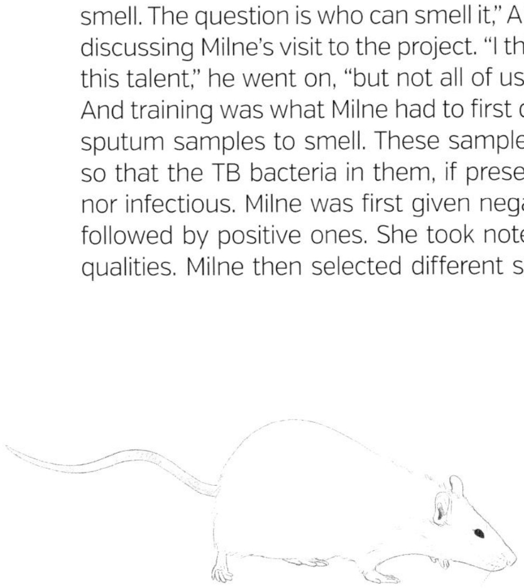

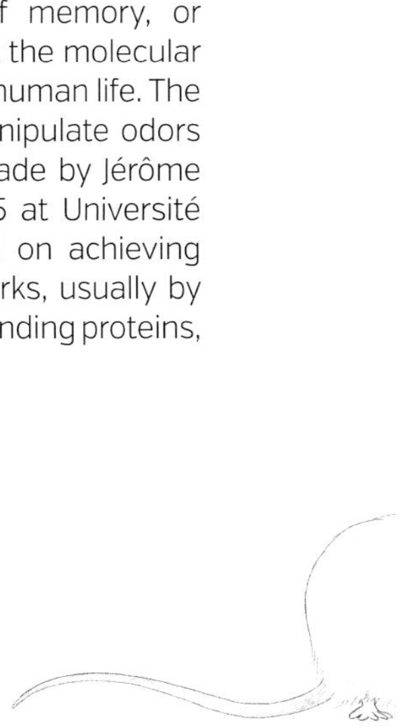

and receptors.[19] "Once you know the molecular mechanisms," the chemist explained, referring to both the molecular structure of odorants and those of odorant receptors, "you can begin to predict how something smells."[20] Yet, this is an ambitious goal. Golebiowski's research uses computational approaches to simulate how odorant molecules might bind to odorant receptors, focusing on the atomic level.[21] He acknowledged that atomic-level models suggest that odorant receptors can distinguish very subtle differences between odorants, and that the reported experience of a smell rarely coincided with any kind of clear structural categorization. There were also genetic factors to consider that result in some people smelling or tasting differently.

In addition to genetic factors, an olfactory experience of an odorant appears to depend on more than just a molecule's structure. Golebiowski highlighted the example of 4-mercapto-4-methylpentan-2-one. At high concentrations, the molecule smells like cat urine; at lower concentrations, it evokes the aroma of cabernet sauvignon or blackcurrant.[22] Mixing two odorants can also trigger a smell that is entirely independent of the addition of its constituents. In some cases, an odorant seems to inhibit a receptor, implying that odor perception is potentially a result of a combinatorial code of both present and absent receptor activity.

Despite these difficulties, the allure to explain and analyze olfaction remains potent, as Sophie Barwich recounts in her book *Smellosophy* (2020). The advent of various technologies for sampling, separating, and analyzing odors as constitutive molecules has only added to this allure. Some of these include Headspace technology, which is a technique for capturing the scent of an object, such as a flower, so that the gas can then be analyzed using gas chromatography–mass spectrometry. Passed through a gas, the extracted scent is separated into its constituent molecular components, distinguished by the different speeds at which each component travels through this gas. These molecular components could then be identified, providing a recipe for the scent that may be recreated by combining these various components. The ability to recreate scents occurring in nature by combining various synthetic compounds lures fragrance companies and artists alike. Once smell has been molecularized, the molecular structures of various substances become the object of further study and elaboration.[23] What molecules give rise to a certain scent? As fragrance chemists would find

16 Yan Li, et al., "Robust Odor Identification in Novel Olfactory Environments in Mice," *Nature Communications* 14, no. 1 (February 13, 2023): 673, https://doi.org/10.1038/s41467-023-36346-x.

17 Alix Spiegel & Elena Renken, "Her Incredible Sense of Smell Is Helping Scientists Find New Ways to Diagnose Disease," *NPR* (March 23, 2020), https://www.npr.org/sections/health-shots/2020/03/23/820274501/.

18 Jules Morgan, "Joy of Super Smeller: Sebum Clues for PD Diagnostics," *Lancet Neurology* 15, no. 2 (2016): 138–39, https://doi.org/10.1016/S1474-4422(15)00396-8.

19 Jérôme Golebiowski, et al., "Interaction between Odorants and Proteins Involved in the Perception of Smell: The Case of Odorant-Binding Proteins Probed by Molecular Modelling and Biophysical Data," *Flavour and Fragrance Journal* 27, no. 6 (2012): 445–53, https://doi.org/10.1002/ffj.3121. See also Uwe J Meierhenrich, Jérôme Golebiowski & Xavier Fernandez, "Les bases moléculaires des premières étapes de l'olfaction," *L'actualité chimique* 289 (September 2005): 29–40, which describes their research as being "from molecule to odor."

20 In conversation with the author (July 10, 2015).

21 Jérôme Golebiowski, et al., "Mechanistic Events Underlying Odorant Binding Protein Chemoreception," *Proteins* 67, no. 2 (May 1, 2007): 448–58, https://doi.org/10.1002/prot.21307.

22 Claire A. de March, "Structure–Odour Relationships Reviewed in the Postgenomic Era," *Flavour and Fragrance Journal* 30, no. 5 (2015): 342–61, https://doi.org/10.1002/ffj.3249.

23 Joachim Schummer, "The Impact of Instrumentation on Chemical Species Identity: From Chemical Substances to Molecular Species," in P. Morris (ed.), *From Classical to Modern Chemistry: The Instrumental Revolution* (The Royal Society of Chemistry, 2002), 188–211; Christy Spackman, "Perfumer, Chemist, Machine: Gas Chromatography and the Industrial Search to 'Improve' Flavor," *The Senses and Society* 13, no. 1 (2018): 41–59, https://doi.org/10.1080/17458927.2018.1425210.

24 Nicola Twilley, "Will Smell Ever Come to Smartphones?" *New Yorker* (April 27, 2016), https://www.newyorker.com/tech/annals-of-technology/is-digital-smell-doomed.

25 Heather Paxson, *The Life of Cheese: Crafting Food and Value in America* (University of California Press, 2013).

out, not all substances extracted from a scent were required to reproduce its signature smell. Indeed, one could recreate complex odors such as feces or a wilting rose with fewer and with synthetic chemical components.

Several engineering and art projects have tried to seize on this technological possibility. Over the years, biomedical engineers, entrepreneurs, and perfumers have come together to create technologies that can send scent by email and a digital scent speaker that can play olfactory playlists.[24] In 2022, the Institute of Contemporary Art at the University of Pennsylvania in Philadelphia hosted *RE________*, in which Norwegian, Berlin-based artist Sissel Tolaas infused and channeled various objects (such as soap and stone), surfaces (walls), ventilation infrastructures, and round-bottom laboratory flasks with smells. One of her works, *SMELLY's_Dark_Secret_22*, features various foul smells including animal odors. Of course, these were not real animal odors. They would have been recreated by first sampling the actual smell and analyzing its constituent molecular compounds, which can then be recomposed using synthetic and other materials.

These projects exemplify the olfactory sublime by eliciting emotions of curiosity, wonder, and amazement, made possible by the various techniques of chemical analyses that enable the composition and curation of smells at the molecular level. Watching people point their noses at smell-emitting holes or flare their nostrils to sniff at a ventilation duct, I noticed how Tolaas's work also points to a moment when the olfactory sublime begins to unravel. What makes her artworks so fascinating is that despite their reliance on molecular techniques for engineering smell, it is really the practice of sniffing, the moment when one's nasal cavities are filled with smell, that remains formidably mysterious to chemists and neuroscientists, yet retains the fascination of perfumers.

1 + 1 ≠ 2

Back in Grasse, I spoke to a group of students learning the art of perfume creation and sensory evaluation at the Institute of Perfumery. Geetha, a perfumer from India, was skeptical of chemical research that tries to understand olfaction. "Sure, it might be useful for understanding physiology or neurology. But it adds nothing to perfumery," she said. In perfumery, "1 + 1 does not equal 2." When I asked her to explain what she meant, she gave me an example of a perfume she had created. The perfume, she said, captured a bright sunny weekend in the markets of Ventimiglia, the Italian town just over the border from the French Riviera. "When you smell this, you think of the Mediterranean, you think of orange blossoms, you think of the red cliffs," she mused. "And I add in a bit of bergamot," she said, turning specific, "not because the perfume has any citrus note, but because I wanted to give it a sparkle."

She sprayed the fragrance on a *mouillette* and handed it to me. I sniffed the air around it. Indeed, it smelled like a bright summer's day by the beach. And as Geetha described, there was a sparkle. It resembled a texture more than a smell. A subtle effervescence that took place in my nostrils, pleasantly tingling like a cool, fresh dip in the sea. "This," she further explained, "is something the chemists can't quite understand yet. What is this feeling? A smell? A sensation? It goes beyond molecular structure." Her colleague, a perfumer from Marseilles, agreed. "Molecular structure provides another language to talk about our materials. But it's just that: terminology to refer to the substances we mix and compose in the lab. It does not explain the art of making perfume," he said. In any smell, there is an endless permutation of ratios and volumes of each odorant. It is almost impossible to know which composition would trigger a receptor. "It is something you must play with, like paint and color. Knowing chemistry doesn't always help," he added as Geetha nodded. I was struck by these perfumers' attunement to the cross-sensory engagement that crafting a smell entails, what Heather Paxson has called "synesthetic reason."[25]

Of course, a chemical or neurological account of smelling would still bring many benefits: the creation of new treatments, the diagnosis of diseases, the design of household products, and the engineering of built environments. But for perfumers like Geetha, these accounts do not adequately explain away the very experience of smelling. "Do you need to know how olfaction works to create perfumes?" Geetha asked. Her question echoed Ally's, the Tanzanian rat trainer, "All these scientists come here to study how rats smell. But do you really need to know that to train rats to detect disease?" They would have both answered "No." The perfumer and rat trainer's questions about smelling defy the molecular, analytical equation of chemical substances and their cascade of receptor and neuronal perception. Seemingly being guardians of the magic of composing odors in perfumery and rat training, Geetha and Ally seem to proffer another kind of olfactory sublime: one steeped in the ethereal quality of smelling.

ELENA GIULIA ABBIATICI
SMELL OF SURVEILLANCE

Elena Giulia Abbiatici is an art historian, researcher, and curator of contemporary art. She has exhibited and developed projects at numerous venues, including the first three editions of "Something Else–Off Biennale" (Cairo), the 56th and 57th Venice Art Biennales, the 15th Venice International Architecture Biennale, the Media Art Festival Maxxi Prize (2016), and Berlin Art Week (2017). Her latest project is "THE ETERNAL BODY: The Human Senses as a Laboratory of Power, Between Climate Crisis and Transhumanism."

+ ART, ART HISTORY

Fragile, open, crossed, hybridized, distilled: the body is immersed in a political field. As Michel Foucault wrote, power relations have an immediate hold on the body: "they invest it, mark it, train it, torture it, force it to carry out tasks, to perform ceremonies, to emit signs."[1] In recent decades, governments, companies, and academic teams have explored the utilization of our unique smells in the realm of surveillance capitalism. Olfactory design has entered the realm of biometric control data, leading to various experiments in this area: machines are taught to capture both the smell of explosives or other dangerous chemicals and the scent of individual citizens.

The link between odors and control is not new. The belief that "good" smells pleasant and "evil" stinks has its roots in Christianity, where the nose became an instrument of moral judgments, capable of filtering good from evil. In the Christian Middle Ages, the personal and Dionysian use of perfumes was condemned, and the official liturgy imposed restrictions on the use of incense and flowers. Social control, and thus control of atmospheres, shifted from the rejection of certain fragrances incompatible with Christian morality to the racialization of body odors, used to assert the superiority of the colonizer and the subjugation of slaves. Today, the application of machine learning in the olfactory sphere allows for computer-based biometric control to profile individuals from their primary odor – the specific odor characteristic of each person, unique and unmistakable, as distinctive and traceable as a fingerprint.

Identifying individuals by their scent has been a longstanding technique used by the police, notably by the East German Secret Police (Stasi) in the 1970s, who secretly collected scent samples. From 1950 to 1990, the Stasi used a series of criteria and means to catalog the odors of people who said or did anything critical of the communist regime in East Germany. In the building where for 40 years the Stasi had its headquarters in the Leipzig district (currently the "Runde Ecke" Memorial Museum), body-scent archives and saliva samples are on display alongside listening and surveillance devices, collections of stolen mail, and covert photographs. In the museum, Section Number 9, Room 109, holds a row of sealed jars, each containing a seemingly innocuous yellow dust cloth, part of the museum's permanent exhibition. Such cloths were used to sample the smell of those who, for example, had distributed leaflets or were caught writing critical graffiti. Placed inside jars, they served to keep track of the specific odors of dissidents.[2] When they found a piece of graffiti or a flyer, Stasi officials would leave a dust cloth to absorb the odor of the subject, covering it with protective aluminum foil. While investigating suspicious citizens, the Stasi employed a variety of methods to obtain their odors, such as breaking into apartments and stealing dirty clothes or seating suspects in a room for questioning and then keeping the yellow cloth hidden under the seat or a strip of fabric from the chair upholstery with the absorbed odor of the suspect's body. Through a trained sniffer dog, the officer then had the opportunity to compare the new odor with the yellow cloth sample kept in the archive. When the target odor matched the test odor, the dog would show a typical conditioned response, usually sitting or lying down, at the target station. If the two odors matched, the Stasi had a concrete name.[3]

It should be noted that the Stasi did not develop odor sampling; it is a well-known police procedure adopted for criminal investigations. A secret patent for odor identification using similar practices was granted in the former German Democratic Republic (GDR) as early as 1972 and was later applied in other countries of the so-called Eastern Bloc. The seriousness of the Stasi's actions lay in tracking the smell of citizens considered subversives as a precautionary measure, not because of the presence of a concrete crime. In a bio-supervised social context, ethical questions arose then, as they arise now: research on computerized olfactory recognition with high-tech sensors continues and is being refined, with a view to flanking other biometric recognition systems, such as iris and fingerprint scanners.

The use of dogs in investigative disciplines has a long history; however, their systematic use in forensics spread mainly during the 20th century, and in the 1980s and 1990s, there was an increase in specialized dog training. It is estimated that the canine sense of smell is 10,000 to 100,000 times better than a human's. If humans have about six million olfactory receptors, dogs have about 300 million. In humans, the olfactory neurons—specialized cells involved in transmitting odor information to the brain—range from 12 to 40 million; in dogs, they can range from 220 million to 2 billion. It is, therefore, not difficult to imagine the extraordinary olfactory capabilities of dogs, making them valuable tools for tracking and searching for missing or runaway persons (even distinguishing between identical twins) or detecting narcotics, poisons, explosives, fire accelerants, and bugs. Despite the widespread use of mantrailing dogs in criminal cases, published rulings specifically addressing the evidentiary value of results obtained through their use are rare.[4] In forensic practice, the results obtained from canine smelling are considered supplementary evidence alongside other conclusive evidence, such as DNA traces, wiretaps, or witness statements. The contribution of mantrailing dogs as primary evidence in criminal cases varies widely internationally. In Germany, the Regional Court of Nuremberg-Fürth in 2012 established strict criteria, requiring the search to be conducted by two independent dogs to strengthen the reliability of the results. In contrast, in France, mantrailing is officially considered more as "technical assistance" than determinative evidence, although the research highlights criminal cases in which human scent identification has been crucial to convictions. In the United States, most states accept mantrailing as tracking evidence, but to ensure widespread adoption, standardized criteria for interpreting results in court need to be established. Increasing the adoption of mantrailing in forensic practice as an evidentiary value would dictate the need for standardized criteria for interpreting their results in court.[5]

Drawing inspiration from the longstanding use of bloodhounds in police work to track and profile individuals, a 2013 study was directed by the Centro de Domótica Integral (CeDInt-UPM) of the Universidad Politécnica de Madrid and partly supported by the Spanish Ministry of Industry and Tourism to explore the computerized identification of individuals based on body odors, a potential biometric identifier in the context of control and security (e.g., borders).[6] It should be noted that body odor can be divided into three components: the primary odor of an individual, which is stable and unchanging over time due to genetic influences; the secondary odor that contains components influenced by diet and environmental factors; and the third odor, which contains components of external and cosmetic origin, including soaps, lotions, and perfumes. It goes without saying that an attempt is always made to extract the primary odor.

In 2009, researchers developed an electronic nose that, combined with a principal component analysis algorithm, can recognize individuals even after the application of a deodorant.[7] In addition, there are further classifications of human body odor: odor from sweating (skin odor), odor released from the oral cavity (exhaled breath, saliva), and odor released from human excreta (urine). The researchers attempted to evaluate the feasibility of identifying people by mass spectrograms of hand odors, according to a machine-learning scheme. Common practice is to divide the data into three subsets: a training set to learn the parameters of the classification model, a validation set to optimize the metaparameters, and a test set for final evaluation. The experimental results, conducted on 13 subjects, achieved recognition rates above 85%, which reveals that there is discriminatory information in hand odors and reinforces the verisimilitude that odor biometrics may be the next biometric technology used in cybersecurity, complementary to other biometric techniques, such as fingerprint and iris recognition. The advantages of odor detection lie in the strong authentication it offers due to the fact that it is currently impossible to replicate body odor. Unlike biometric techniques such as facial recognition, which has a high error rate, and fingerprint technology, which requires contact, odor biometrics offers high accuracy without contact.[8] There remains, however, a percentage shortfall. Will it be filled? What technique will assure us a total, secure, reliable, and accurate recognition rate in the near future?

Ethical issues arise due to the invasiveness of such technology, as it captures highly personal information. The possibility of individuals being identified based on their body odors may have limitations on freedom of movement and participation in public, civic, and political life. If our odor signatures serve the control and security industry, it is not difficult to imagine forms of discrimination based on ethnic or gender characteristics as interpreted by an algorithm. Misuse of biometric odor data, such as the production of inaccurate results, will inevitably generate injustice, false accusations, or discrimination. The difference between possibilities for greater security and risks of privacy violations, moreover, is something that depends on the situation in which each person finds themself.

In recent years, a number of artists have grappled with the dystopian horizon of biometric odor control. These include the Russian art collective Where Dogs Run, which, in its installation *Faces of Smell* (2012), analyzes surveillance capitalism through the explorations and investigations that the smell of our bodies and breath can potentially trigger. Gas detectors and analyzers are placed in tubes that are part of the installation to collect information about people, their locations, and their biology. When a person approaches the gas analyzer and sniffs the tubes, the tubes sniff in turn. Once the air composition data is processed, it is compiled and produces a face – a witness to their presence at that moment. A person sees a face that conforms to their smell. While not physically matching the face of the subject being analyzed, the face that emerges is the algorithmic result of a combination of physiognomic features drawn from an archive of police identikit that the artists fed to the algorithm in a further operation of subverting the supervisor–supervised roles.

If the goal of big tech companies is to be able to unlock our iPhones with our olfactory signature, by contrast, the smell device devised by Dutch designer Leanne Wijnsma and the filmmaker Froukje Tan is designed to alert internet users instinctively of data leaks from their personal devices – the alter egos of our bodies. The inspiration for this work is driven by the addition of mercaptan to gas following the tragic explosion of a school in New London, Texas, caused by a gas leak on March 18, 1937: gas, in fact, is a dangerous substance without smell. Similarly, data also have no scent. As several privacy breach incidents show, data leaks can have serious consequences. Building on this connotation, Wijnsma developed *Smell of Data* (2014) and chose to use the sense of smell because it is directly connected to the brain and can invoke action almost instantly. A fragrance suitable for data reporting was created in collaboration with the company Scent Air after a long study of the effects of various fragrances and numerous tests on essences. This new fragrance contains essences of iodine, a kind of metallic fragrance well associated conceptually with data and technology, and essences of citrus, known to promote recall action almost instantly.

Continuous data mining will eventually lead individuals to put in place countersurveillance strategies to avoid leaks of genetic material, which could lead to the commercialization of databases or an instrumentalization of them in the name of a genetic class to be targeted if necessary for military and biopolitical purposes. Transdisciplinary artist and educator

1 Michel Foucault, *Discipline and Punish: The Birth of the Prison* (Giulio Einaudi Editore, 2014), 29. Originally published as *Surveiller et Punir, Naissance de la prison* (Gallimard, 1975).

2 Runde Ecke Museum, "Section 9: Room 109," www.runde-ecke-leipzig.de/ (accessed December 7, 2023).

3 Kate Hairsine, interview with Tobis Hollitzer, "Stasi Surveillance," *DW* (May 23, 2007), https://www.dw.com/en/the-stasi-had-a-giant-smell-register-of-dissidents/a-2555053.

4 Agata Kokocińska-Kusiak, et al., "Canine Olfaction: Physiology, Behavior, and Possibilities for Practical Applications," *Animals (Basel)* 11, no. 8 (2021): 2463.

5 Leif Woidtke, et al., "The Use of Mantrailing Dogs in Police and Judicial Context, Future Directions, Limits and Possibilities – A Law Review," *Forensic Science International: Synergy* 7 (2023): 100439.

6 Irene Rodriguez-Lujan, et al., "Analysis of Pattern Recognition and Dimensionality Reduction Techniques for Odor Biometrics," *Knowledge-Based Systems* 52 (2013): 279–89.

7 C. Wongchoosuk, M. Lutz & T. Kerdcharoen, "Detection and Classification of Human Body Odor Using an Electronic Nose," *Sensors* 9, no. 9 (2009): 7234–49.

8 Sameena Naaz, et al., "OdorTAM: Technology Acceptance Model for Biometric Authentication System Using Human Body Odor," *International Journal of Environmental Research and Public Health* 19, no. 24 (2022): 16777.

9 Heather Dewey-Hagborg, "Hacking Biopolitics," *e-flux conversations* (February 2017), https://conversations.e-flux.com/t/heather-dewey-hagborg-hacking-biopolitics/6045.

10 Heather Dewey-Hagborg, "Sci-Fi Black Crime Drama with a Strong Black Lead," *The New Inquiry*, https://thenewinquiry.com/sci-fi-crime-drama-with-a-strong-black-lead/. no. 9 (2009): 7234–49.

Above: Heather Dewey-Hagborg, *Stranger Visions,* Installation: Found genetic materials, custom software, 3d prints, 2012-2013.

Heather Dewey-Hagborg's work *Invisible* (2013), developed as an open-source workshop and promotional video for two complementary genetic privacy sprays, accompanies the laboratory research conducted to prepare two gaseous mixtures that can be used to remove traces of DNA hidden, for example, in our saliva. In the video, 108 nanograms of DNA contained in one microliter of saliva are hidden and removed by two "Erase" and "Replace" flasks, which obscure all remaining DNA. The artist has also arranged protocols for a DIY realization of the aforementioned sprays, offered by the imaginary biotechnology company BIOGENFUTURES, which she founded. Technically speaking, the Erase spray, composed of bleach and water, would erase 99.5% of DNA, while Replace would replace the remaining 0.5% biological material with a derivative of 50 different DNA sources. The artist's attempt is to propose an open-source method for obfuscating biological data, an iconoclastic artistic gesture of countersurveillance intended to ignite reflection on the vulnerability to which bio-surveillance exposes us. The artist wonders: could it be so simple to hack DNA evidence, so simple that just a few ingredients and procedures that can be implemented in a standard kitchen would be enough?

Could it be easy, the artist again provokes, to circumvent single DNA profiling with a DNA spoofing operation, which, like IP spoofing–a particular type of attack that allows a malicious actor to conceal their identity in order to appear trustworthy to the intended victim–can confuse authorities and render physical trajectories anonymous? In the video *DNA Spoofing* (2013), a still camera captures Dewey-Hagborg and developer and programmer Aurelia Moser scrambling genetic material, surrendering to each other strands of hair, chewing gum, traces of lipstick taken directly with a sample from each other's mouths, eyelashes, and fingernails. The artist shows a do-it-yourself technique to counter genetic surveillance and confound its tracking and reconstruction from the genetic material that we constantly disperse.

Fallen hair, cigarette butts, chewing gum, glasses with traces of saliva and fingernails are some of the artifacts she obsessively collected from 2012 to 2013 for another of her art projects, *Stranger Visions*, to examine as much as she could about the people who dropped them. By combining bioinformatics and machine learning tools, she was able to draw statistical inferences or predictions about how they looked physiognomically, how they behaved, and what the health conditions were of the unknown individuals whose DNA she had collected. Dewey-Hagborg eventually simulated a 3D representation of their genetic data, appropriating some techniques to create full-color, life-size 3D portraits, prompting a heated debate about the possibilities offered by genetic surveillance. The disruptiveness of the work was evident: from the halls of art, it shook the conscience of many and infiltrated mass media, social media, and public policy on genetic privacy.[9]

In December 2014, the year following the conception and production of *Stranger Visions*, forensic DNA phenotyping (FDP) would make headlines when the company Parabon NanoLabs began offering law enforcement agencies across the United States a service called "Snapshot," capable of producing a descriptive profile of any human DNA sample, predicting physical characteristics including skin pigmentation, eye and hair color, facial morphology, sex, and genomic ancestry. The future that the artist envisioned with *Stranger Visions*, having stepped outside the confines of artistic lucubration, would turn out to be a disturbing reality, generative of danger and concern at the judicial level. At present, there appear to be no legal rules governing the use of unvalidated forensic technologies. It is becoming increasingly alarming because of the distortions that phenotyping technology, still unreliable and biased, may produce in criminal investigations.

Although FDP cannot take into account age, environmental influence on genetic expression, or individuals' decisions to embrace an identity that is not biologically determined or to alter their appearance through diet, hair color, contact lenses, makeup, hormones, or plastic surgery, the more pressing and real risk here is that the use of these technologies, nurtured by computational averages, may feed into the genetic classification system of individuals, and justify gender and racial stereotyping. It is therefore feared that identity categories such as biogeographical ancestry, reduced to algorithms, in the hands of police and bio-tech companies, will become a form of racial profiling, supported by the apparent authority of DNA science. While the concept of race lacks a genetic basis, a realization underscored after the Holocaust and reiterated following the Human Genome Project, scientists can artificially construct it by associating extensive genetic datasets with traditional racial classifications. Sociologist Troy Duster refers to this tendency to seek correlations implying race while simultaneously refuting its existence as the "molecular reinscription of race."[10]

The power exercised over the body produces knowledge (data), and this knowledge produces power relations that render human bodies objects of economic extraction and control. Whoever is subjected to a field of visibility, writes Foucault, despite not knowing whether the overseer is present in the observation tower, will exercise behavioral control on themselves. The prison cell of the digital panopticon is a place from which, as in Plato's cave, the prisoner does not even have the possibility to escape. Every second, the digital tower surveys and captures the digital shadows of the body prisoners reflected on service clouds, disseminated and traceable everywhere. When we breathe, walk, or sleep, everything becomes an olfactory source that can be captured by surveillance devices. The panopticon constantly changes form but not essence. We are continually faced with the possibility of dispersing bodily traces in public, leaving physiologically capturable and decodable artifacts. We are identified without contact, without awareness, and without fail by the odors we carry with us.

LISA YIN HAN

AQUATIC LIVING SENSORS AND THE MAKING OF COMMON SENSE

Lisa Yin Han is an assistant professor of film and media studies in the English Department at Arizona State University. Her research is situated at the intersections of environmental media studies, critical ocean studies, and science and technology studies. Her current book project, *Deepwater Alchemy: Extractive Mediation and the Taming of the Seafloor,* examines how media operations in deep ocean environments pave the way for extractive industries.

+ MEDIA STUDIES, SCIENCE + TECHNOLOGY STUDIES

What if the US government were funding a clandestine unit of marine organisms to work as underwater spies and security guards? Though it may sound like the plot of an *Aquaman* sequel, this is no Hollywood fantasy; this is a very real, ongoing investment by marine biologists, engineers, and the state. Launched in 2018 and now in its second phase, the Persistent Aquatic Living Sensors (PALS) program is a research program funded by the Defense Advanced Research Projects Agency (DARPA) to leverage the communication signals of aquatic animals in the service of military undersea surveillance.[1] Defense contractors such as Raytheon, Northrop Grumman, the Naval Undersea Warfare Center, and others have partnered with researchers around the country to study and test the viability of transforming species such as the Goliath grouper, black sea bass, snapping shrimp, and bioluminescent plankton into low-cost, discreet, military sensors to detect underwater vehicles.

Militarization and instrumentalization of aquatic wildlife, particularly for surveillance, have a precedent in Cold War-era studies of cetaceans, underwater sound, and even bioluminescent plankton and microorganisms. As media historians like John Shiga and Max Ritts have demonstrated, marine biologists and the US Navy have a long history of collusion that has brought us to our present-day ability to travel and mediate the deepest part of the seas.[2] However, recent projects like PALS are not just conducted with national security in mind; they also interface with industrial efforts to build underwater monitoring systems, as well as environmental research on human disturbances to ocean ecologies. As territorial behaviors and courtship sounds are remediated through smart algorithms, data sets, and digital aquariums, the use of underwater living sensors is becoming increasingly infrastructural, impacting ocean knowledges across many different social and political spheres.

How do we account for the cultural, economic, and institutional entanglements that have made underwater living sensor networks plausible? My aim is to reflect on these emergent ecologies of technology alongside both cultural representations of the ocean and what Jake Kosek terms the "ecologies of empire," referring to the ways in which sovereign power capitalizes on natural ecologies.[3] In particular, I draw on frameworks from environmental media studies and sound studies to bring attention to how processes of mediation mobilize interspecies couplings within existing social structures of power. Critiquing the utilitarian orientations of the living sensor program as well as its accompanying representations of marine life, I argue instead for a return to "common sense," which I define as a sense of being-in-common that foregrounds humility, mutual interdependence, and solidarity across species lines.

Listening to Nature

The PALS program is marketed to the public as a noble effort to "listen to nature."[4] But the "nature" in question is hardly as simple or as expansive as the statement's appeal. Ideas of nature are framed by technology as well as by existing environmental ideologies that subjectively position nature as background, as default, and as separate from the human world. DARPA project manager Lori Adornato echoes this perspective in her introduction to PALS: "At the moment we treat all this natural sound as background noise, or interference, which we try to remove. ...Why don't we take advantage of these sounds, see if we can find a signal?"[5] Adornato describes the project as an attempt to recuperate wasted sound, equating "noise" with waste and "signal" with sounds that are deemed useful or profitable to humans. But reducing this complex process of sorting sound to "listening to nature" ignores the specificity of who is doing the listening and why.

Defining an animal as a sensor or a guard depends on a social, technological, and economic structure that legitimates their participation in human systems. These conditions frame what researchers are listening for, for whom they are listening, and who gets to do the listening. While living sensors may be used for a variety of purposes, underwater surveillance networks are designed and developed with particular ideas in mind about what matters and what does not matter, and how to interpret or present the collected data. These choices comprise a culturally informed technique of listening that organizes information, isolates the senses, and objectifies data according to a desire for "an identifiable order in the resonant world" of the oceans.[6]

First, the species selected to be a part of the PALS surveillance system must have specific attributes, such as wide distribution and easily detectable communication signals (either they are very loud or very bright). Aggregating multiple acoustic techniques, PALS researchers then use a suite of sensing tools and algorithms to listen specifically for the presence of underwater vehicles. This consists of sonar-based techniques that detect the echoes that are produced when grouper calls or shrimp snaps and their sounds reflect off hard surfaces. The proposed method repurposes some of the sonar techniques that are already widely in use in our oceans, while machine learning is added to help to deduce the location of the sound source and the vehicle, and then to categorize the type of sound the animals produce. Grouper Guard's Principal Investigator Laurent Chérubin explains that detecting underwater vehicles requires establishing a baseline of a typical audiovisual landscape or biological soundscape, and then training an algorithm to identify what is "suspicious," "out of place," or a "potential threat" for the species in question.[7]

As is evident in Chérubin's statement, the nature that is being listened to is wrapped up in a narrow set of considerations that both center questions of national security and collapse human security concerns with animal security concerns. Although the living sensor surveillance system is listening to animal stress signals, these signals are determined in relation to an ideal human subject, which, in this case, is the state. This is not, for instance, a listening for pain, a listening for desire, or a listening for relations. The fish, the shrimp, and the plankton become technological proxies and part of the sensing system, while the targets or underlying objects that are being *listened for* are human made: a sound signature of a ship, a submarine, or an underwater drone.

Besides the Navy, PALS researchers also imagine other listeners that are part of their shared research networks, who typically include both environmental scientists and contractors for industrial offshore extraction. The environmental applications of living sensors have already been promoted widely to the public. As activities such as transoceanic commerce, drilling, war, and global warming alter the natural chatter of the seas, climate scientists describe changing animal soundscapes as warning systems for the planet, repurposing similar language to PALS as well as the technical methods used by those hoping to design an animal and AI-based surveillance system for defense.[8] On the flip side, to underscore the idea that living surveillance systems are hands-off and innocuous to the environment, PALS uses terms like "spying," "eavesdropping," or, to use the more technical term, "passive acoustic monitoring."[9]

This passive, nature-friendly language is misleading. Hearing the grouper calls requires implementing a physical infrastructure consisting of hydrophones and other underwater sensors that are capable of picking up on grouper or shrimp sounds. Ironically, this infrastructure enables the very industries and activities

1 DARPA Outreach, "DARPA's PALS Program Enters Second Phase," Defense Advanced Research Projects Agency (September 29, 2020), https://www.darpa.mil/news-events/2020-09-28.

2 Max Ritts & John Shiga, "Military Cetology," *Environmental Humanities* 8, no. 2 (2016): 196–214.

3 Jake Kosek, "Ecologies of Empire: On the New Uses of the Honeybee," *Cultural Anthropology* 25, no. 4 (2010): 650–78.

4 David Hambling, "Why the US Military is Listening to Shrimp," BBC (June 16, 2022), https://www.bbc.com/future/article/20220616-the-new-sonar-built-from-sealife-noises.

5 Quoted in Ibid.

6 Jonathan Sterne, "Mediate Auscultation, the Stethoscope, and the 'Autopsy of the Living': Medicine's Acoustic Culture," *Journal of Medical Humanities* 22, no. 2 (2001): 130.

7 Gisele Galoustian, "How Goliath Groupers Behave May Be the Key to National Security Under the Sea," Florida Atlantic University (February 20, 2019), https://www.fau.edu/engineering/news/1902-goliath-groupers/.

8 Woods Hole Oceanographic Institution, "As Oceans Warm, Snapping Shrimp Sound a Warning," WHOI Press Release (August 18, 2022), https://www.whoi.edu/press-room/news-release/as-oceans-warm-snapping-shrimp-sound-a-warning/.

9 Tim McMillan, "DARPA Will Use Marine Life to Spy on Enemy Subs," *The Debrief* (March 16, 2021), https://thedebrief.org/darpa-will-use-marine-life-to-spy-on-enemy-subs/.

10 Hambling, "Why the US Military is Listening to Shrimp."

11 Lisa Han, *Deepwater Alchemy: Extractive Mediation and the Taming of the Seafloor* (University of Minnesota Press, forthcoming).

12 Naval News Staff, "DARPA's PALS Aims at Detecting Undersea Activity Thanks to Marine Organisms," *Naval News* (February 19, 2019), https://www.navalnews.com/naval-news/2019/02/darpas-pals-aims-at-detecting-undersea-activity-thanks-to-marine-organisms/.

13 Galoustian, "How Goliath Groupers Behave."

14 Nat Geo WILD, "Amazing Pistol Shrimp Stun 'Gun,' | World's Deadliest," YouTube (April 11, 2013), https://www.youtube.com/watch?v=KkY_mSwboMQ; Henry Joost & Ariel Schulman (dirs) *Project Power* (Netflix, 2020); Katie Carman, "Pistol Shrimp: The Fastest Gun in the sea," *How Stuff Works* (May 5, 2021), https://animals.howstuffworks.com/marine-life/pistol-shrimp.htm.

15 Ann Elias, *Coral Empire: Underwater Oceans, Colonial Tropics, Visual Modernity* (Duke University Press, 2019); Jon Crylen, "Cinema Cnidaria, or Marine Movies in an Age of Mass Extinction," *Media Fields Journal* 13 (2018).

16 The term "naturecultures" was coined by Donna Haraway in *The Companion Species Manifesto: Dogs, People, and Significant Otherness* (Prickly Paradigm Press, 2003).

17 Kendra Coulter, *Animals, Work, and the Promise of Interspecies Solidarity* (Palgrave Macmillan, 2016), 155–56.

that exacerbate sonic pollution in our oceans. One *BBC* article on PALS by David Hambling states these seemingly contradictory environmentalist and extractive aims in the same paragraph: "Tuning in to the sounds made by normal marine life, and learning how they change, would give researchers a low-cost, environmentally friendly way of tracking the impact of human activities underwater. This would be useful for projects like off-shore wind farms, oil drilling, and seabed mining."[10] While the underwater surveillance structure itself might have a relatively small environmental impact, clearly the same cannot be said for offshore wind farms, oil drilling, or seabed mining.

Hambling's reference to minimizing cost and human labor also speaks to values that have historically informed the development of undersea media technology. Indeed, oceanographic research institutions have been referencing the same potential applications of underwater media technology for decades, invoking environmental science, national security, offshore industry, and a desire to lower costs in order to fund the development of other key underwater technologies such as side-scan sonar, seismic imaging, and autonomous underwater vehicles, which are used for a wide range of activities including marine science, industrial prospecting, and nautical archaeology.[11]

Importantly, although these uses of living sensors are often referenced together, they are not ranked equally. Behind every proposal is a footnote: the US Navy will receive the PALS technology before anyone else, and "if DARPA identifies any of the data, results, or technical specifications as controlled unclassified information, DARPA will require the PALS researchers to protect them to prevent proliferation outside of official channels."[12] So on the question of who we are listening for, the answer is quite evidently a selective group of people in power. The rest–scientists, groupers, shrimp–receive only what trickles down.

Fantasies of Interspecies Power

As techniques of listening, living sensors are also themselves represented in culturally specific terms. Take, for instance, this opening line from a press release on the Grouper Guard project: "They're stealthy, territorial and naturally dominant. That's why the exceptionally large Goliath grouper [*Epinephalus itajara*] is the focus of a novel smart-sensing system that will remotely alert authorities of incoming manned and unmanned underwater vehicles."[13] The article goes on to compare groupers to barking guard dogs - language that socializes animals as inherently violent and militaristic.

Many of these militarized imaginaries of aquatic life have associations beyond the PALS project. For example, snapping shrimp are well-known by their alternate name, "pistol shrimp," and they are often represented in terms of their speed ("the fastest gun in the sea") and predatory behavior in nature documentaries, science communication efforts, and even science fictional films like Netflix's *Project Power*, which repackages shrimp speeds into a superpower-granting pill.[14] Major studios like Disney, Warner Bros., and 20th Century Studios have also contributed to militarized imaginaries of the sea, as fish-riding warriors from *Aquaman* to *Avatar* further entrench fantasies of animal complicity in military power. These popular representations of undersea space as belligerent are nothing new. Media historians have charted tropes of undersea violence in relation to a colonial Western gaze since the advent of underwater filmmaking in the early 1900s.[15]

As is evident from press releases, technical literature, and other media about aquatic living sensors, programs like PALS calcify a particular set of values and imagined futures in their very conceit. Following the interventions by feminist science studies and environmental scholars such as Donna Haraway and Stacy Alaimo, it is common in the environmental humanities to turn to notions of "naturecultural"

18 Adam Fish, "Crash Theory: Entrapments of Conservation Drones and Endangered Megafauna," *Science, Technology, & Human Values* 46, no. 2 (2021): 425–51.

19 Isabelle Stengers, "We Are Divided," *e-Flux Journal* 114 (December 2020), https://www.e-flux.com/journal/114/366189/we-are-divided/ (emphasis added).

20 Astrida Neimanis, "Bodies of Water, Human Rights, and the Hydrocommons," *TOPIA: Canadian Journal of Cultural Studies* 21 (2009): 178.

21 Debbora Battaglia, "Cosmos as Commons: An Activation of Cosmic Diplomacy," *e-Flux Journal* 58 (October 2014): 3.

hybridity and human–nonhuman collaboration as an antidote to harmful, anthropocentric perspectives on wilderness.[16] However, multispecies and more-than-human formations today are far from a monolith. As Zipporah Weisberg argues, human and nonhuman hybridity is not inherently liberatory, but rather is subject to late-capitalist logics, as is evident in the militarization and industrialization of living sensors. Weisberg's critique is valuable here most simply in its underlying attention to historical and material conditions. That is to say, we cannot reduce or ignore the political, economic, and institutional formations that produce these hybrid technologies in the first place.

In this case, there is a need to consider the complex positionality of the fish and shrimp spy as alternately victim, disposable worker, manifestation of empire, and media infrastructure. Living sensors enable and enact existing cultures around sensing, even when they are implemented for altruistic aims such as marine conservation or climate change research. When we talk about groupers as guards and shrimps as pistols rather than as stressed animal communities, we are making choices to socialize nonhuman life in a way that invites their exploitation. In spite of these enclosures of animal sensoriums, there is a potential to think further about the labor of animal sensors in a way that pays attention to shared interspecies socialities—both those that emerge from conditions of vulnerability and those that emerge from positions of power and privilege.

Interspecies Diplomacy

Reflecting on animal labor, Kendra Coulter advocates for the development of interspecies solidarity as a way of pushing back against representations of animals as tools, taking seriously the way in which labor impacts animal bodies and feelings: "we must not only consider work, but also work-lives, and lives, period."[17] Brought into a system as cheap workers, yet excluded from the rights and dignities of citizenship, snapping shrimps and Goliath groupers occupy a political positionality not unlike marginalized communities in the human world. Perspectives on multispecies justice can therefore benefit from recognizing synergies with existing notions of labor justice, economic justice, epistemological justice, and racial justice.

Ideas about interspecies solidarity also complicate dominant frameworks for environmental advocacy that produce relationships of dependency between marine ecologies and human interventions. These relationships of dependency are evident not only in systems like PALS, but also in the rise of other technocratic environmental solutions. For instance, cultural anthropologist and interdisciplinary scholar Adam Fish charts a similar dynamic around conservation drones, arguing that "endangered people, like endangered species, are becoming reliant upon drone power," describing both as forms of systemic, technological entrapment.[18] Rather than defer to environmental advocacy perspectives that exacerbate tendencies toward technological dependency and the objectification of animals, we might be better served by pivoting to a framework of diplomacy, which requires and is based on relationships of interdependence between human and nonhuman stakeholders.

What then, does an interspecies diplomacy consist of? Writing on diplomacy, Isabelle Stengers contends, "what diplomacy requires—the ability of a group to ponder the way it formulates obligations, its ability to *make common sense* of what maintains it and what it has to maintain—is precisely what has been undone by chains of dependence."[19] I want to build on Stengers's mobilization of the term "common sense" here, as both a common sense of obligation to others and a sense of being-in-common that speaks to the multispecies political possibilities of the ocean commons itself. Commoning includes ideas about democracy, local governance, and distributive justice, as well as a sense of a multispecies justice. Going a step further, environmental scholar Astrida Neimanis has suggested that the idea of a "hydrocommons" might help us to take into account the physical qualities of water itself, its capacity for crossing borders, and the symbiotic existence of all bodies of water. She writes, "the common does not stop at our skin. ...As the gestational matter of our being, water also expresses our actual responsibility and our virtual potential."[20] Interspecies diplomacy in the context of our oceans thus requires a common understanding of this responsibility and a potential for multispecies coexistence.

Another affordance of diplomacy is its ability to allow for the interaction of multiple knowledge systems. In her cosmic theorizations of diplomacy, Debbora Battaglia defines "geontological diplomacy" as a mode of worldbuilding that "enjoins us to hear not only what natural entities might have to tell humans in their own terms, and vice versa, but [also] to study how nature-culture differences might be scaled to purpose."[21] Battaglia's elaboration helps us to expand the positionality of the listener as well as the listened-to, beyond the scale of the human. When we see underwater media technologies as technologies of diplomacy rather than of warfare, we augment their capacity to service the hydrocommons as a whole rather than merely reinforcing existing power dynamics that benefit a minority in power.

There can be no doubt that with the multiple streams of investment around AI, underwater sensing, and ocean surveillance technology, living aquatic sensors will play a part in our ocean futures. However, their environmental and political possibilities have yet to be determined fully. Perhaps if they are developed with common sense in mind, they may yet serve a future beyond the top-down enclosures that loom on the horizon.

DOUGLAS ROBB

LISTENING TO LANDSCAPE

Douglas Robb is an assistant professor of landscape architecture at the University of Calgary School of Architecture, Planning, and Landscape. Doug's research centers on the production of just and inclusive climate futures using place-based methods of drawing, writing, and designing. Doug holds a PhD in geography from the University of British Columbia and a master's degree in landscape architecture from the University of Toronto. He was previously the inaugural Ian McHarg Fellow at the University of Pennsylvania Stuart Weitzman School of Design and a Research Fellow at the Canadian Centre for Architecture.

+ SOUND STUDIES

In the summer of 2021, as I was preparing for my PhD fieldwork, my supervisor, Karen Bakker gave me a copy of *Sound and Sentiment* by the American anthropologist Steven Feld.[1] At first, this book seemed like an odd choice. First published in 1982, *Sound and Sentiment* explores the soundscapes and acoustic life of the Kaluli people of Papua New Guinea. My fieldwork, on the other hand, aimed to study the social and environmental impacts of a controversial new hydroelectric dam in northern British Columbia, Canada. For my fieldwork, I planned to conduct extensive landscape observation and documentation through drawing and photographs, utilizing my eyes rather than my ears. Karen's gift was welcome, but also confounding: how was an acoustic ethnography based halfway around the world relevant to my research on Canadian energy landscapes? What lesson or insight was she hoping to impart by giving me this book?

In retrospect, I understand that Karen was trying to persuade me to reconsider the importance of sight in my work, and to guide me toward different ways of engaging with landscapes through my other senses—particularly my sense of hearing. At the time, the value of this approach was not apparent to me. But, since then, Karen's wisdom has reshaped my approach to studying and engaging with landscapes. Her insights have encouraged me to explore the auditory dimensions of our environment, recognizing that sound, too, plays a crucial role in how we experience and understand the world around us.

Karen Bakker sadly passed away in the summer of 2023. This article, framed in her memory, reflects on some of the lessons she taught me. I use this space to review one of her final books, *The Sounds of Life: How Digital Technology Is Bringing Us Closer to the Worlds of Animals and Plants*, and to explore its relevance to design.[2] In doing so, I speculate on the transformative (and, in my view, underdeveloped) role of sound in landscape architecture.

Through this exploration, I hope to honor the legacy of Karen's work and to argue for its potential to influence the development of our discipline profoundly.

The Sounds of Life

The Sounds of Life delves into the hidden world of sonic landscapes, also known as soundscapes. We can think of soundscapes in terms of simultaneous and overlapping layers of sound from different sources: geophony, biophony, and anthrophony. Geophony encompasses the sounds of natural physical processes, such as wind, rain, and geological activity. These sounds form the acoustic backdrop against which all other sounds occur. Biophony includes the sounds produced by nonhuman biological organisms, like birdsong, insect chirps, and whale calls. These sounds are critical indicators of the health and biodiversity of ecosystems. Anthrophony, on the other hand, refers to the sounds generated by human activities, including both beneficial sounds, like music, and detrimental impacts, such as noise pollution from industrial activities.

The Sounds of Life emphasizes the importance of listening closely to our environment, including sounds that occur beyond humans' auditory range. To access these previously inaudible soundscapes, the book investigates recent advances in the emerging field of digital bioacoustics. Using tools such as ultrasonic microphones and underwater hydrophones (among many others), bioacousticians can capture and analyze sounds that are otherwise imperceptible to the human ear. *The Sounds of Life* catalogs many of these innovative listening technologies–and the researchers behind them–to investigate how sound can be a powerful tool for environmental monitoring and conservation. For example, the analysis of bird songs can provide insights into the presence and abundance of certain species, offering knowledge of the biodiversity of a landscape; likewise, the monitoring of underwater sounds can reveal information about marine life, which can then be used to guide human activities, such as the reduction of shipping traffic and its associated noise in the presence of migratory whales.

The interplay among digital bioacoustics, environmental sensing technologies, and recent advances in machine learning and artificial intelligence holds the potential to transform the design and governance of landscapes radically. These technologies can help to enhance ecological and biodiversity values when directed toward efforts such as habitat conservation, landscape restoration, renewable energy deployment, and other pro-environmental causes. But the act of listening also carries certain practical and conceptual risks; like the predatory colonial gaze, digitally enhanced hearing can be used as a form of biopower, opening up new frontiers of passive surveillance, control, and exploitation. Digital tools can enhance humans' listening capabilities, but they can also distance us from direct, unmediated sensory experiences. The need for digital technologies to access these soundscapes raises questions about experiential authenticity.

In exploring these complex dynamics, *The Sounds of Life* invites us to recognize and reflect upon the often-overlooked auditory dimensions of landscapes. This is particularly relevant for landscape architecture, in which sonic engagement with the environment has been historically overshadowed by visual approaches. Emphasizing sound challenges us to rethink our familiar research and design practices and to consider how other senses can deepen our understanding of landscapes in more ethical and inclusive ways.

Ethical Listening

Landscape architecture has traditionally prioritized vision as the primary sense through which to analyze and engage with the environment. The ocularcentric nature of our discipline can be traced, in part, to its origins in landscape painting and related visual practices.[3] Yet overreliance on visual conventions rooted in European representational techniques can result in the marginalization of other forms of situated environmental knowledge, including non-Western perspectives and spatial traditions.[4] Despite a growing awareness of and appreciation for multisensory design, contemporary design education and practice continue to rely predominantly on visual tools, metrics, and modes of representation.[5]

Listening, like seeing, is not a neutral act. Just as the colonial gaze has been used to dominate and control landscapes, listening can also be wielded as a form of biopower to regulate and control populations. For instance, A. M. Kanngieser argues that the act of listening can be complicit in processes of dispossession and control, echoing colonial practices of surveillance and dominance typically associated with Eurocentric visuality.[6] By exploring the colonial dimensions of sound, Kanngieser draws attention to the asymmetrical power dynamics inherent in the act of listening, which can unintentionally perpetuate historical injustices and obscure forms of Indigenous sonic knowledge. Paul J. Guernsey similarly discusses how the infrastructures of settler colonialism—such as increasingly ubiquitous environmental sensing technologies—can shape humans' sensory perceptions and interactions with the environment in ways that enable extractive relationships.[7] The act of rendering landscapes audible and knowable through digital technologies risks reducing complex ecological systems to mere data points, stripping away their intrinsic value and agency. In the absence of proper oversight and governance, digital bioacoustics may not, in fact, catalyze a new era of multispecies communication and collaboration, but rather deepen human domination and exploitation of nonhuman life.

This is not to suggest that landscape architecture is disinterested in non-visual ways of sensing and depicting landscapes, or that engaging with the sonic dimensions of space is inherently damaging. As Dell Upton argues, auditory experiences play a fundamental role in shaping human environmental perceptions and values.[8] Listening offers a mode of attunement toward landscape that can help to transcend landscape architecture's reliance on optical information. However, the continued dominance of sight in landscape architecture (and other design practices) can limit human engagement with the full sensory dimensions of place and can exclude other forms of cultural and place-based knowledge.[9] *The Sounds of Life* invites us to reconsider this visual bias and to integrate sound as a vital component of landscape architecture design. In doing so, it calls on designers to create environments that are not only visually appealing, but also sonically rich and ecologically responsive.

Listening to Landscape

To counteract these potential pitfalls, landscape architects must recognize the social and ethical responsibilities inherent to the act of listening. Designing with soundscapes requires specific practices of attunement and care, but what might these approaches look like? How can we learn to listen to landscapes in just and ethical ways?

The Sounds of Life argues that deep listening involves more than passive hearing; rather, it is an active and intentional practice. Soundscapes are embedded in specific contexts, shaped by particular biophysical and socioecological interrelationships. Hence, the act of listening is also always a situated and embodied act that requires the listener to become attuned to the sonic relationships of place. Put another way: "If we want to engage in authentic communication with nonhuman beings, we also need to cultivate a relationship with the places and the ecological communities they inhabit."[10] As I learned during my

Bowhead Whale

Coral Reef

PhD fieldwork, this usually means moving slowly and quietly – a pace that is often at odds with the tight timelines imposed by academic and professional practice. Soundscapes are powerful venues for storytelling and socioecological memory, and the subtle sounds of a place can reveal hidden histories and narratives.[11] However, to hear these stories, one must first learn to be silent while also recognizing the diverse senses through which humans and nonhumans experience and interact with their environment.

The act of listening can enrich traditional visual modes of design practice by offering new ways for designers to encounter the nonhuman world sonically. The advent of digital bioacoustics has greatly expanded humans' ability to perceive and analyze soundscapes. Tools such as distributed acoustic sensors and digital sound mapping offer new ways to listen to nonhuman soundscapes, revealing the previously overlooked auditory capacities of plants and animals. For example, recent developments in the emerging field of soundscape ecology have demonstrated how these technologies can be used to document the biodiversity of ecosystems through their acoustic signatures.[12] Auditory sensing technologies function like digital translation devices, enabling us to perceive and interpret soundscapes that were previously inaudible.[13] By extending our sensory capacities, acoustic monitoring can reveal patterns of wildlife activity, detect changes in ecosystem health, and even track the impacts of climate change.[14] Landscape architects can then use these data to inform design decisions that support biodiversity and ecological resilience.[15] Rather than relying on visual indicators to assess ecosystem health, designers might integrate bioacoustics sensors into their projects, providing a continuous stream of rich and informative ecological data.

Digital bioacoustics can enable our ears to become our eyes–a potentially radical proposal for design disciplines

1 Steven Feld, *Sound and Sentiment: Birds, Weeping, Poetics, and Song in Kaluli Expression* (Duke University Press, 1982).

2 Karen Bakker, *The Sounds of Life: How Digital Technology is Bringing us Closer to the Worlds of Animals and Plants* (Princeton University Press, 2022).

3 Dianne Harris & D. Fairchild Ruggles (eds), *Sites Unseen: Landscape and Vision* (University of Pittsburgh Press, 2007).

4 Daniel A. Friess & Tariq Jazeel, "Unlearning 'Landscape'," *Annals of the American Association of Geographers* 107, no. 1 (2017): 14–21.

5 Daniel Roehr, *Multisensory Landscape Design: A Designer's Guide for Seeing* (Routledge, 2022).

6 A. M. Kanngieser, "Sonic Colonialities: Listening, Dispossession, and the (Re)making of Anglo-European Nature," *Transactions of the Institute of British Geographers* 48, no. 4 (2023): 690–702.

7 Paul J. Guernsey, "The Infrastructures of White Settler Perception: A Political Phenomenology of Colonialism, Genocide, Ecocide, and Emergency," *Environment and Planning E: Nature and Space* 5, no. 2 (2022): 588–604.

8 Dell Upton, "Sound as Landscape," *Landscape Journal* 26, no. 1 (2007): 24–35.

9 Juhani Pallasmaa, *The Eyes of the Skin: Architecture and the Senses* (John Wiley & Sons, 2024).

10 Bakker, *The Sounds of Life*, 177.

11 Keg de Souza, "Pedagogies of Place: Listening and Learning in the Margins," in Tatiana Flores, Florencia San Martín & Charlene Villaseñor Black (eds), *The Routledge Companion to Decolonizing Art History* (Routledge, 2024), 218–27.

12 Bernie Krause, *The Great Animal Orchestra: Finding the Origins of Music in the World's Wild Places* (Little, Brown and Company, 2012).

that have traditionally prioritized sight. Beyond mere passive acts of digitally mediated listening, these technologies allow designers to engage with landscapes in new and novel ways. For example, sound can serve as a marker of social and environmental justice issues. Noise pollution often disproportionately affects marginalized communities (including nonhuman communities), leading to adverse health outcomes and reduced wellbeing.[16] By addressing these issues through sound-informed design, landscape architects can contribute to better policies and environments that mitigate the negative effects of noise and promote healthier, more inclusive soundscapes. Media theorist Shannon Mattern similarly emphasizes the importance of multisensory engagement–including listening–as an essential mode of landscape research and analysis.[17] Mattern discusses how our sensory experiences are mediated by technologies and cultural practices, and how these experiences shape our understanding of space and place. Fostering a deeper understanding of humans' connection to their local soundscapes can encourage designers to engage with communities in a more meaningful and inclusive manner, and to develop proposals that better reflect the specific sonic contexts they inhabit.

The integration of digital technologies in sound studies has not only transformed our understanding of human-wildlife communication; it has also led to significant advancements in our understanding of how plants talk to each other. A number of recent studies have shed light on the ways in which trees communicate with one another through chemical signals transmitted through mycorrhizal networks or via terpenes released into the air.[18] However, the auditory capacity of plants has remained relatively under-investigated. Researchers such as Monica Gagliano have recently explored how plants use sound waves to interact with their environment and other organisms.[19] Gagliano's experiments in the nascent field of phytoacoustics have shown that plants can detect sound, create sound, and develop behavioral responses to specific sound frequencies, suggesting that they have a form of sonic perception. For instance, her experiments have shown how plants' roots will grow toward the sound of running water, even when the water is isolated behind a waterproof membrane. This research challenges the traditional view of plants as passive entities and highlights their role as active agents that can both respond to and shape their environments – information that has long been known by Indigenous peoples.[20] By acknowledging the acoustic life of plants, previously inaudible without bioacoustics technologies, landscape architects can design environments that support and enhance these interactions.

Conclusion

The Sounds of Life offers a profound reflection on the sonic dimensions of our world, challenging us to rethink the sensory hierarchies that have shaped landscape architecture and allied design disciplines. The book calls on us to embrace listening as a mode of attunement and a practice of care that can transcend the discipline's reliance on optical information. By integrating sound into our design practice, we can create landscapes that are not only visually beautiful, but also sonically vibrant and ecologically rich. However, this positive outcome is not necessarily guaranteed; to co-create truly just and inclusive soundscapes, we must learn how to listen to landscapes in ways that avoid the harmful pitfalls of visuality. This will require conscious effort on the part of designers, scientists, and policymakers to ensure that technological innovations in digital bioacoustics are not co-opted by entities seeking to exploit and capitalize on this new frontier of multispecies communication.

Listening to landscapes offers a path toward a more inclusive and ethically attuned practice of landscape architecture – one

African Elephant

Amazon River Turtle

that listens deeply to the world around us. This work involves not just the incorporation of sound into our designs, but also a fundamental shift in how we perceive and communicate with our environments. Embracing the full spectrum of sensory experiences can enable the creation of spaces that are more resilient, sustainable, and reflective of the diverse voices and rhythms of the natural world. One of the greatest gifts Karen gave me was the reminder to close my eyes and open my ears to the Earth's whistles, trills, gurgles, groans, croaks, and roars – to the vibrant sounds of life that surround us. Let us honor her memory by creating landscapes that are not only seen but also heard, felt, and experienced in their full sensory richness.

13 Bakker, *The Sounds of Life*, 41.

14 Max Ritts & Karen Bakker, "Conservation Acoustics: Animal Sounds, Audible Natures, Cheap Nature," *Geoforum* 124 (2021): 144–55.

15 William M. Adams, "Geographies of Conservation II: Technology, Surveillance and Conservation by Algorithm," *Progress in Human Geography* 43, no. 2 (2019): 337–50.

16 Erica D. Walker, et al., "Descriptive Characterization of Sound Levels in an Environmental Justice City Before and During a Global Pandemic," *Environmental Research* 199 (2021): 111353.

17 Shannon Mattern, *Code and Clay, Data and Dirt: Five Thousand Years of Urban Media* (University of Minnesota Press, 2017).

18 Richard Karban, "Plant Communication," *Annual Review of Ecology, Evolution, and Systematics* 52 (2021): 1–24; Francesco Loreto & Sabato D'Auria, "How do Plants Sense Volatiles Sent by Other Plants?," *Trends in Plant Science* 27, no. 1 (2022): 29–38; Suzanne Simard, *Finding the Mother Tree: Uncovering the Wisdom and Intelligence of the Forest* (Penguin Random House Canada, 2021).

19 Monica Gagliano, *Thus Spoke the Plant: A Remarkable Journey of Groundbreaking Scientific Discoveries and Personal Encounters with Plants* (North Atlantic Books, 2018).

20 Janelle Marie Baker, "Do Berries Listen? Berries as Indicators, Ancestors, and Agents in Canada's Oil Sands Region," *Ethnos* 86, no. 2 (2021): 273–94; Robin Wall Kimmerer, *Braiding Sweetgrass: Indigenous Wisdom, Scientific Knowledge, and the Teachings of Plants* (Milkweed Editions, 2013); Vanessa Watts, "Indigenous Place-Thought and Agency Amongst Humans and Non Humans (First Woman and Sky Woman Go On a European World Tour!)," *Decolonization: Indigeneity, Education & Society* 2, no. 1 (2013).

IN CONVERSATION WITH MARK PETER WRIGHT

Mark Peter Wright is a London-based artist and writer whose creative use of sound and documentary media explores the relationship between the field and the studio, and between observers and the observed. His work combines sound, installation, writing, and performance, creating a shared space for sensing and sense-making while amplifying forms of power and poetics. Karen M'Closkey spoke with Wright about his latest book, *Listening After Nature: Field Recording, Ecology, and Critical Practice* (2022), wherein he examines field-recording practices, and troubles our assumptions about the sounds of nature and the nature of sounds.

+ Has the use of sound always been a key part of your artistic practice, and if so, how has its role in your work changed?

I studied film over 20 years ago, which introduced me to sound as a creative, critical medium. It helped me to understand that sound can be an art form, that sound is design, that sound matters. It opened up a new world, and I eventually found my way to field recording and soundscape studies that, like film, dealt with similar ideas of assemblage and construction. As time went on, I moved away from thinking about the compositional aspect of editing and zoomed in on the practice of recording as a site of inquiry. My attention shifted toward the recorded encounter, toward the ethical and aesthetic knots that are embroiled when we point a microphone at something, whether a human, an object, or an animal. In some ways I consider my pathway a typical route – you begin being quite enamored with a medium, with sound, and then you gradually become more aware of what you are doing with it, and why. Sound is not simply artistic material; it is a teaching medium, a critical probe, a sensibility.

+ At the beginning of *Listening After Nature*, you reference the Anthropocene and ongoing sixth mass extinction, noting that humans have been both destabilized and reaffirmed in this context. This serves as a prompt for thinking about how field recording practices must be interrogated in terms of the presence of the person doing the recording. Can you elaborate?

The book is guided by the question "what am I not hearing?" It is the inverse of the obvious question, which is "what are we hearing in the soundtrack?" To lean the ear toward things that we might not hear is an inherently political question. One of the answers to the question, what am I not hearing, is found in the glimpses and traces of the person doing the recording. Field recordists are curious creatures. We often negotiate self-silence. We tread quietly, we move in slow motion, we try to suppress back pain, or not to rustle leaves underfoot. That drive to be silent is part of an inherited division between subject and object, signal and noise.

Aesthetically, recordists are often sidelined as an unwanted artifact within the recording. Self-silencing can take place for all sorts of reasons, but I'm interested in what lurks in the material and conceptual space of that quiet possibility. That's how and where the figure of what I call the noisy-nonself emerged. That persona is a reconfiguration of the field recordist. It is the thing that lurks in the hiss of media – the shuffles and bumps of representation. The noisy-nonself is a prompt for practice. It is a productive interference that I hope can embolden practitioners to think critically and creatively about how agency is negotiated in the field, and in the audio document itself, as well as their own selves. I wouldn't want to promote a culture of sonic selfies or anything like that – it is not just about saying "I'm here," but more of a speculative, ethical space for tuning attention toward fieldcraft and decision making as well as offering something to listen for when auditioning field recording-based works in the studio, classroom, or gallery.

+ In nature documentaries, viewers would likely presume that what they are hearing is a field recording that happened concurrently with the video recording of the same scene, yet you describe the prevalent use of Foley artists (named after early 20th-century sound artist Jack Foley). In what ways does it matter that what we are hearing is not what we are seeing, especially if we are not aware of that fact?

Foley is the art of post-production sound effects. The difficulty of capturing sound on location provides this kind of rationale for recreating the sound in the controlled environment of the studio, or the Foley stage as it's known. The Foley stage is where the aesthetic renderings come together to enhance perceptions of time, space, weight, size, texture, these sorts of things. It is a fascinating and vital element of film. I take it very seriously as an art form. There is immense craft and knowledge about objects and recording techniques that go into these works. These artists understand how sound is linked to our perception and memory of actions and events.

Foley methods are routinely employed in wildlife documentaries. For example, the microscopic world of butterflies is recreated with almost comedic techniques, like the flapping of gloves or the flick of a comb. Those recordings are then taken into a computer and manipulated to produce the sound effect. The stakes are quite high, I suppose, with nature documentaries. There is a presumed veracity in terms of knowledge production. The fact that 90% of that sound design is fake doesn't necessarily mean it is problematic, unless there is a very extreme case of appropriation going on. Being aware of that might change how we listen and might, therefore, change how we come to know something.

+ The phrase "seeing is believing" means we trust our eyes more than our ears. You suggest that this presumption is a productive space within which to work – you call it "sonic fiction." Can you give an example?

Lawrence Abu Hamdan's *Earwitness Inventory* (2018–ongoing) is a great example. He really shows the potential of Foley if we take it seriously as an art form. He custom designs objects that are connected to earwitness testimony from legal cases – people describing sonic events through similes, often evoking materials or effects that have nothing to do with the actual sonic thing that was happening, for example someone might describe a building collapsing like the sound of popcorn. It is a powerful disjuncture that pulls at reality, pulls at memory. I find it ironic that something fictional can move us closer to understanding real circumstances. It is not necessarily a truth or fact that will do that but sometimes it is this other layer.

We can certainly think of a field recording not as an object, but a kind of kaleidoscope of interpretations based on all the things we've spoken about. The sound recording is always in a status of being questioned in terms of its truth and validity, which is a great space to play in as an artist and researcher. I often speak about critical play, which is something I like to do in my work and teaching. Play is not just fun; it is also necessary and serious.

+ Returning to animal recordings, you wrote about the extinct ivory-billed woodpecker. All that is left is a field recording from 1935. You mentioned that these recordings are like ghosts. Do you think it is important we have such artifacts?

Yes, it is incredibly important to have these artifacts. It is important to conserve and make accessible things that are no longer here. Bound up in that heritage project is the politics and practices of its production. The salvage paradigm of Western science is tied into colonial processes and hierarchies of knowledge that often omit why such preservation is needed in the first place. It is not so much about the bird's voice as a rare object, or a sonic taxidermy, but how that voice, that object, can be reimagined and rethought through the context in which it operated, and to consider how that can have resonance today. That is the difficulty with these things. A lot of natural history museums have to have trophy species to lure people in. It's all the networks and politics around the recording that you hope are being reanimated as well.

+ The flipside is that we not only record nature; it also "records" us, as in the examples of the lyrebird and bowerbird, the former made famous in a David Attenborough documentary when it reproduced the clicking sounds of the camera (though the actual sound could have been Foley). You say that mimicry offers potential for artistic practices that complicate field recording. Can you give an example?

I think of bowerbirds as more-than-human field recordists. They can play back the sounds of their environment immediately, which is quite an uncanny skill, a multi-linguistic skill. What I learned from mimicry is that it can be an art form that adds versions of reality to the existing slices of reality that are out there. When we hear lyrebirds, or bowerbirds, mimicking chainsaws, we know something is not quite right. It is not a perfect copy. It prompts this thinking, feeling, listening practice that you can return to again and again because you hear the fallibility of truth in the recording. I do this a lot with students. The bowerbird recording is incredible to play, and to try to listen with, and to think about what is actually going on.

This mimicry connects back to Foley. I've always loved the detail that you can bring to thinking about the weight and texture of things. A dog's footsteps are often made by someone wearing leather gloves (or boxing gloves for evoking a large dog) and having paperclips on the ends of their fingers. Rain is bacon being fried. Grass under foot is shredded paper, and the sound of a thunderstorm is tinfoil. These large-scale events are sonically perceived through mundane materials. If we think of those things as an art form, we should be able to scrutinize them. In an age of disposable plastics, what does it mean to seek out a sustainable mimicry practice or Foley practice, where perhaps materials are ethically sourced, or we only use those that are recycled? This type of limit could be very productive.

+ You described an artist who embedded microphones into dead birds and recorded other birds feasting on their flesh. I perceived this as a critique of representations that present nature as benign but you also said it is not as simple as that. Why?

There is a well-known recording by Chris Watson called *Cracking Viscera* where mics were placed on a carcass as vultures swooped and tore at it. It is an incredible document, yet it splits the audience. It provides a close-up insight into this visceral world of the animal kingdom, but there is always an ethical discussion that surfaces about placing the microphones in a carcass. I think this method is mirrored in nature documentaries where there is literally bait being used – they set up a carcass and wait for things to happen to film it. I am not making a moral judgment at all. It is an audio document that I think will always be prone in terms of its ethics, which is why it's fascinating.

I'm interested in fieldcraft as much as the recorded documents. What were the decisions being made? What microphones and why? Where is the author? Can we hear the technology media in the account? These are simple questions, but they are ones that I like to work with. So going back to this question about what we are not hearing in the example of the carcass is that the recordings are in Kenya. There are clearly shadows of safari hunts and safari conservation, a place where hunters, tourists, and scientists have historically crossed paths. Preservation and predation are always nested together. That is what makes the track so interesting for my students. The aim is about how much listening we can pour into that track and what strategies, questions, knowledge, or critiques can arrive out of it.

+ In your book, you highlighted the artist Peter Cusack, who recorded himself walking through oil fields. How does this compare to photographers like Edward Burtynsky who create beautiful and disturbing images of similar places? Some say this type of work aestheticizes the ravaged landscapes, while others argue that the beauty of the images is what initially captivates us, only to shock us when we realize what the subject matter is. How does this dynamic shift when the medium is sound?

The sound recording is from his project called *Sounds from Dangerous Places*. It is called an oil field sound walk. When you listen to the track, you're placed into the embodied ears of the recordist who is recording with in-ear binaural microphones as they walk through an oil field full of monotonous mechanics and drilling. It is a very embodied sense of place rather than a top-down bird's-eye view, like in the work of Burtynsky. I'm trying not to set up a dichotomy between sound and image because I think both have their nuances and limitations. Sound is a very temporal situation. The sonic scene, if you like, is incredibly dynamic and embodied. Probably less static than the image; perhaps even more relational through its ambulatory perspective. Acoustic knowledge is a very felt knowledge. I like to think that listeners can transpose themselves into that environment, like an extra shadow of the recordist. If I look at an image, I can visually transpose myself, yet there is a palpable sense of embodiment and transportation that happens through sound. In this particular recording, because the artist is wearing microphones in their ears, you get a left-right kind of perspective of what is going on. Sound is itinerant. It is always on the move. We often hear what we can't see. There is a lot of room for interpretation for truths, plural, to emerge within that kind of openness, and that will always connect to an ethical discussion because of sound's capacious nature.

+ It seems that we can look at an image and not imagine a sound, but it would seem incredibly difficult to listen to sound and not conjure images about what we think we are hearing. There is a lot of imagination on the part of the listener. I would think that titles are incredibly important for setting the context for listening.

That is something that I talk about in *Listening After Nature*. When I come together with students to listen to these works, it is a strange process of assembling meaning or interpretation. It is a very partial, fragmented jigsaw puzzle. I wouldn't want to recreate a pictorial scene. It is not show and tell, but you do build up a picture of sorts, and there are bits and pieces of it missing. It has an openness that I just spoke about. The danger, of course, is exactly what you say about context, such as the sonorous allure of the oil field, where I might think about it as some kind of musical composition without considering the impact on land and communities. Cusack recognizes this paradox in his reflections on the work. *Sounds from Dangerous Places* is a very pragmatic title; his project is a book with sound, images, and text. I find it interesting to stress test the limits of what we can know without certain bits of context. Then what happens when we have them? How does our listening change when we repeatedly listen with more layers of meaning?

+ We've discussed recording sounds that are available to the human range of hearing. What about sounds that fall outside of that range? Has that opened up a new world or new material that is being interestingly explored by artists?

Yes, for sure, artists are really tapping into this new material world – part of a vibrational ontology of practice where sound and its energies and affects are being prioritized. These kinds of works fall into what I call "elsewhere fields." They are part of our everyday lives, and yet we cannot always access them. The whole animal world is full of sound beyond the human range of hearing, which is 20 to 20,000 Hertz. We are granted temporary access to these worlds through specialist microphones and techniques – hydrophones, bat detectors, VLF recorders, all sorts of wonderful things. I think listeners are being encouraged to participate in a world that is radically not theirs to know. It is a strange space to hear as a listener. But we can't dwell in that world forever. We get kicked back out into our limited bandwidth of experience. It is important to acknowledge those differences; to recognize that, for all our technology, we'll never know what it is like to be in that world. That is a good thing, I think. It also begs the question, maybe we shouldn't know or try to know everything there is to know. Perhaps some sounds are better off left in the sea or the air.

+ I appreciated your comment that, as problematic as the history of recording practices is, *not recording* is not the answer. Did you take a break from recording and, if so, what brought you back?

I did. But I don't want to be seen as a Luddite, or an anti-tech person, or to suggest that listening is somehow more appropriate than recording. It's not. Everything is full of complex, knotty issues. I stopped recording for a few years due to a physical problem with my back. I couldn't walk very well for a long time. I couldn't carry equipment. It made me reflect on the ableism that drives field recording. I started to think about my own body as a site of study and I started to appreciate small-scale, hyper-local projects. That brought me back to recording in a different way. The pause renewed my interest in the ethics of capture. It made me want to build a practice that focused on the practice of listening and recording. The key mantra for me is to keep pressing record. It is not about hanging up the microphones, it is about how to record otherwise.

+ In addition to recording, you speak about how to listen. What is "slow listening?"

Sound demands a durational commitment of the audience, of the auditor. I am constantly listening to some very strange recordings with my students. Some sound works might be 40 minutes long. You think, "Can I really take up this time within a 3-hour class?" Actually, one should. You can't really get a conventional snapshot of sound. That is the trick of slow listening, I suppose, or encouraging slow listening in a kind of pedagogical sense to accommodate that demand of sound so that its aesthetic and ethical content can be drawn out. It is very different when we do that together. Then as a collective, we try to make sense out of what just happened. We need that, and time, and space.

+ Your book ends on a note of optimism. You say that critical practices should not just tear things down but must involve hope, which, and you quote Susan Sontag, "arrives out of uncertainty." How would you define uncertainty in this context?

I am inspired by research that doesn't work in a deficit mode or drag a negative critique throughout. A lot of hope comes from the studio, and the classroom from working with students. I remember a session a few years back where we were talking about sound and extinction and a lot of the students went into a strange vortex where they said, "What's the point?" To hear the bowerbird as it vocalizes anthropogenic sounds is quite crushing in many ways. To think about the damage that's going on in the planet and the human incursion that's going on everywhere. At the same time, I'm keen to try to keep some sort of affirmation alive within everything that I do. These birds are incredibly virtuoso, sentient, aesthetic creatures that occupy and produce a world that I could never be a part of, and I don't understand at all. There's a vibrant agency there, not just mourning or a lament.

There is a very palpable hope gap where students feel increasing anxiety or hopelessness around issues like social justice and climate damage, and that the actions being taken are not adequate for the task ahead. I am not trying to fill that gap. I am trying to build some sort of steppingstones that might lead to some more affirmative and critical spaces. I think uncertainty is bound up in that journey. Sound is always full of uncertainty for the reasons we've touched on, and that makes it a very productive space. I really appreciate the minor or incidental sounds that we don't necessarily seek out, whether it's recording in the field or listening back to a piece. There is uncertainty in the process of audition, which offers clues to what is going on. Uncertainty presents multiple possibilities and perspectives. That for me is quite a hopeful place to be.

SENSESCAPES

DAVID HOWES

The certainty of the philosopher Immanuel Kant's conception of "the bounds of sense" as informed (or delimited) by the *a priori* categories of time and space, and his claim that "the mind makes the object," were plunged into doubt in the wake of the phenomenological turn. For example, in *Phenomenology of Perception* (1945), Maurice Merleau-Ponty insisted on the unity of mind and body and thereby pulled the rug out from under Kant's transcendental subject.[1]

The Kantian conundrum was exacerbated further by the sensory turn in the human sciences, inspired by anthropologist Paul Stoller's concept of "sensuous scholarship," historian Constance Classen's idea of the "cultural history of the senses," and geographer Paul Rodaway's notion of "sensuous geographies".[2] The latter turn redirected attention to the "sensory underpinnings" of thought and the multiple respects in which the "sensorium" is best understood as a historical formation. In effect, the senses both filter our perception of the world and make the mind.[3]

The concept of the sensorium is foundational to the interdisciplinary field of sensory studies. In the opening chapter of *The Varieties of Sensory Experience* (1991) entitled "The Shifting Sensorium," Jesuit polymath Walter J. Ong defines the sensorium as "the entire sensory apparatus as an operational complex," and goes on to state that "differences in cultures...can be thought of as differences in the sensorium, the organization of which is in part determined by culture while at the same time it makes culture."[4] The term sensory studies was coined in 2006 to denote the convergence by a range of disciplines—anthropology, history, and geography—on the sensorium as an object of study.[5] This confluence resulted in the break-up of the monopoly that the disciplines of philosophy and psychology had formerly exercised over the study of the senses and perception. As philosopher/theorist Michel Serres presciently remarked in 1993: "If a revolt [in our figurations] is to come, it will have to come from the five senses!"[6] Serres might well have been predicting the birth of sensory studies.

Incidentally, the sensory turn also problematized the phenomenological turn. In the *Phenomenology of Perception*, the emphasis is not only on the unity of mind and body, but also on the "prereflective unity" or "synergy" of the senses. According to Merleau-Ponty, "my body is a ready-made system of equivalents and transpositions from one sense to another. The senses translate each other without any need of an interpreter, and are mutually comprehensible without the intervention of any idea. ... Synesthetic perception is the rule."[7] Sensory studies scholars challenge this unitary understanding of the sensorium by pointing to how the senses may conflict as well as coalesce, as in the example of the stick half in water (which looks crooked to the eye but feels straight to the touch), or the opposition between "the male gaze" and "the female touch"—that is, the division of the sensorium along gender lines.[8] These scholars maintain that the centrifugal tendencies of the sensorium deserve no less attention than the centripetal or so-called synesthetic.

David Howes is a distinguished research professor in the Department of Sociology and Anthropology, co-director of the Centre for Sensory Studies at Concordia University, and adjunct professor of the Faculty of Law at McGill University, Montreal. He is a legal anthropologist, a pioneer of the anthropology of the senses and a leading theorist in the interdisciplinary field of sensory studies. Publications include *The Sensory Studies Manifesto* (2022) and *Sensorial Investigations* (2023).

+ SOCIOLOGY, ANTHROPOLOGY

By way of illustration of the notion that the senses make the mind, consider psychologist Rudolf Arnheim's claim in *Visual Thinking* (1969). There he argued that thinking should be regarded as a continuation of seeing, rather than coming first. Tellingly, however, Arnheim dismissed the cognitive potential of the non-visual senses: "One can indulge in smells and tastes, but one can hardly think in them."[9] The anthropological record contradicts this claim. Consider the olfactory cosmology of the Ongee, an Indigenous people of the Andaman Islands, whose mode of subsistence centers on hunting and gathering. Their categories of time, space, and personhood are all mediated by olfaction. The Ongee calendar is "a calendar of scents," in which each season is named after the most odoriferous flower that blooms during the corresponding period. The space of the village fluctuates depending on the activities that go on within it; for example, it expands olfactorily when people cook pork. When Ongee persons refer to themselves, they will point to their nose. The smell of sweat is considered to be an emanation of the soul or life force, which is most concentrated in the bones. The Ongee take great care to manage their body odor–such as by painting the body with clay to prevent it from escaping–because, if they do not, the "greedy" ancestral spirits who are odorless (being without bones) will abstract their scent (i.e., devour their soul), which leads to sickness or death. So too with hunting game animals–the Ongee engage in an elaborate game of olfactory hide-and-seek with their prey.[10]

Other examples of such *sensuous epistemologies* include the acoustemology of the Kaluli people of Papua New Guinea and the thermal dynamics of the Tzotzil of Mexico.[11] The acoustic takes precedence over the visual in Kaluli epistemology. The closeness of the rainforest environment makes it difficult to see very far, and open views are rare. Avian symbolism plays a key role in Kaluli culture and aesthetics. For example, there are many stories of humans turning into birds. Because birds are heard more often than they are seen, the Kaluli are adept at bird-listening, rather than birdwatching: they classify different species of birds onomatopoeically by the sounds they make (rather than their plumage), and in their calls the Kaluli hear the voices of the ancestors. Acoustic motifs such as "lift-up-over sounding" (the sound of a waterfall) pervade Kaluli ceremonial life; for example, they never sing in unison, much less harmony, rather, each singer's voice lifts-up-over those of others in a never-ending cascade.[12]

The thermal cosmology of the Tzotzil of the Chiapas Highlands of Mexico is exemplified by the way they classify the cardinal directions and celestial bodies by reference to temperature: the East is called Rising Heat, the West Waning Heat, and the Sun is Our Father Heat. People are classified by temperature: "men are believed to possess more heat than women, making women symbolically cold by contrast."[13] Plants, too, are classified according to heat. For example, corn is hot because it grows above ground, toward the sun, while potatoes are cold because they grow underground. Similarly with colors: red signifies heat and black coldness. As anthropologist Claude Lévi-Strauss observed in *Wild Thought* (1962) regarding the classificatory schemes or "science of the concrete" practiced by such peoples as the Ongee, Kaluli, and Tzotzil, sensible qualities are "good to think with."[14] Thus, Arnheim was out of line. Classen presses further:

> When sensory orders express cosmic orders, cosmologies are not only read about or heard of, but lived through one's own body. Every time a Tzotzil woman walks on the cool earth with her bare feet she is reminded of her symbolic coldness. The Tzotzil feel their cosmology through the temperature of their bodies, the Ongee breathe in theirs with every breath. …These sensory cosmologies make us aware of the many different ways in which culture shapes perception, and the inability of standard Western models to comprehend such sensory and symbolic diversity.[15]

These cosmologies make "worlds of sense" in Classen's terminology. It would appear there is a world of difference between the sensuous epistemologies and sensory cosmologies or sensescapes sketched above and the abstractions of modern physics.[16] Quoting A. N. Whitehead, Classen has observed how advances in physics transformed the cosmos from a vibrant universe of sense throughout the premodern period into "a dull affair, soundless, scentless, colourless; merely the hurrying of material, endlessly, meaninglessly" in modernity.[17] But we do not wish to tarry on the alleged eclipse of the senses brought on by modern physics, or the technologization of perception (by means of the telescope and microscope) that preceded it, or the reduction of sensation to "information" or "data" in contemporary cognitive science, since enough ink has been spilled on these topics.[18] In any event, the reality is more complex. Indeed, if anything, the life of the senses has intensified in modernity, not receded. As Caroline A. Jones observes in "The Mediated Sensorium":

> The human sensorium has always been mediated. (Without the 'medium' of air or water, the anthropoid ear finds it impossible to hear.) But over the past few decades that condition has greatly intensified. Amplified, shielded, channeled, prosthetized, simulated, stimulated, irritated – our sensorium is more mediated today than ever before.[19]

She goes on to express the hope that "we can come to feel the body pulsing" in tandem with all the extensions of the senses by means of technology, "that we can learn to partner our proliferating technologies in increasingly coordinated, supple and critically conscious ways."[20]

Following Jones's call, we need to lower our sights from the far reaches of the galaxy (mediated by the electron telescope) and raise our sights from the atomic level (mediated by the electron microscope) to train *all* of our senses on the "distribution of the sensible," the "politics of the perceptual" and the modulation of the senses

1 Maurice Merleau-Ponty, *Phenomenology of Perception* (Routledge & Kegan Paul, 1962 [orig. 1945]).

2 Paul Stoller, *The Taste of Ethnographic Things: The Senses in Anthropology* (University of Pennsylvania Press, 1989); Paul Stoller, *Sensuous Scholarship* (University of Pennsylvania Press, 1997); Constance Classen, *Worlds of Sense: Exploring the Senses in History and Across Cultures* (Routledge, 1993); Constance Classen, *The Color of Angels: Cosmology, Gender and the Aesthetic Imagination* (Routledge, 1998); Constance Classen (ed.) *A Cultural History of the Senses* (Bloomsbury, 2014); Paul Rodaway, *Sensuous Geographies: Body, Sense, and Place* (Routledge, 1994).

3 This filtering goes on not only at the cultural level (as per Ong), but also at the psychophysical level.

4 Walter J. Ong, "The Shifting Sensorium," in David Howes (ed.), *The Varieties of Sensory Experience* (University of Toronto Press, 1991), 28.

5 M. Bull, P. Gilroy, D. Howes & D. Kahn, "Introducing Sensory Studies," *The Senses and Society* 1, no. 1 (2006): 5–7.

6 As quoted in David Howes, *The Sensory Studies Manifesto* (University of Toronto Press, 2022), 3. See also Michel Serres, *La Legende des Anges* (Flammarion, 1993).

7 Merleau-Ponty, *Phenomenology of Perception*, 235, 229.

8 Classen, Ch. 3 "The Scented Womb and the Seminal Eye" and Ch. 4 "Pens and Needles," in *The Color of Angels*; see further Ch. 9 in Martin Jay, *Downcast Eyes: The Denigration of Vision in Twentieth-Century French Thought* (University of California Press, 1993) on Luce Irigaray's critique of Merleau-Ponty.

9 Rudolf Arnheim, *Visual Thinking* (University of California Press, 1969), 19.

10 Classen, *Worlds of Sense*, 126–31; C. Classen, D. Howes & A. Synnott, *Aroma: The Cultural History of Smell* (Routledge, 1994), 137–38, 143–48, 152–55.

11 Steven Feld, "Places Sensed, Senses Placed: Toward a Sensuous Epistemology of Environments," in David Howes (ed.), *Empire of the Senses* (Routledge, 2005); Tom Rice & Steven Feld, "Questioning Acoustemology: An Interview with Steven Feld," *Sound Studies* 7, no. 1 (2021): 119–32; Classen, *Worlds of Sense*, 122–26.

by diverse technologies.[21] The sensuous scholarship of Stoller, Classen, Rodaway, and Jones herself, among others, has led the way in this direction. What follows is a brief exploration of how this quickening of the senses has also taken root within the history, theory, and practice of architecture, urban planning, and landscape architecture.

The 2005–2006 *Sense of the City: An Alternative Approach to Urbanism* exhibition at the Canadian Centre for Architecture (CCA), curated by then director Mirko Zardini, is a good point of departure. Zardini could have divided the exhibition space along conventional sensory lines, with one area devoted to seeing the city, another to hearing the city, and so forth, but he thought better. Instead, one room was devoted to illumination (celebrating the work of Linnaea Tillett) and cartography (including tactile, Braille maps); another featured a living wall of plants (to evoke the idea of the lungs of the city) and a row of decanters containing the essence of freshly baked bread and garbage for visitors to sniff. A third room, inspired by the work of R. Murray Schafer and the *World Soundscape Project*, was strewn with bean bag cushions where visitors could recline, don a pair of headphones, and eavesdrop on the everyday sounds of London, Paris, and Buenos Aires streamed live. A fourth room documented the ice palaces of Québec City during Carnaval and snow-clearing in Montréal–a massive logistical operation that generates mountains of dirty, gray cleared snow in the dumpsites. The *pièce de résistance* was given over to documenting the "second skin of the earth" – namely asphalt, its texture (there was a piece of bitumen visitors could handle), and colors (e.g., tinted patches, road markings). It was noted how paving city streets (instead of using cobblestones) reduced dust and eliminated friction, thereby smoothing the way for urban traffic and upping the velocity of transport.

In the introductory essay to the *Sense of the City* catalog entitled "Toward a Sensorial Urbanism," Zardini proposes that a new term, "sensorial urbanism," be added to the litany of definitions assigned to contemporary urban planning (new urbanism, post-urbanism, re-urbanism, everyday urbanism, eco-urbanism, etc.).[22] All the latter terms, he suggests, were lacking an ineffable something – namely, the senses and sense. Zardini goes on to recuperate the work of a range of theorists and activists from the 1960s and '70s, including Kevin Lynch and Jane Jacobs, who had gestured toward this sensory lack and attempted to correct it. He then adduces how "city planning has long privileged qualities of urban space based exclusively on visual perception," abetted by the twin drives of hygienization and standardization, which marginalized and sought to suppress unwanted smells and sounds. He makes note of a "renewed interest in a sensorial experience extending beyond the visual realm" within contemporary architecture, as exemplified by the work of Juhani Pallasmaa, Steven Holl, and Kengo Kuma.[23] Zardini's essay concludes with a paean to such

12 Steven Feld, *Sound and Sentiment: Birds, Weeping, Poetics and Song in Kaluli Expression*, 3rd ed. (Duke University Press, 2012).

13 Classen, *Worlds of Sense*, 123.

14 C. Lévi-Strauss, *Wild Thought: A New Translation of La Pensée Sauvage*, trans J. Mehklman & J. Leavitt (University of Chicago Press, 2021 [orig. 1962]); also see C. Lévi-Strauss & D. Eribon, "Sensible Qualities," in P. Wissing (trans), *Conversations with Claude Lévi-Strauss* (University of Chicago Press, 1991), 110–15.

15 Classen, *Worlds of Sense*, 136.

16 Feld, "Places Sensed, Senses Placed"; Classen, *Worlds of Sense*; Classen, *The Color of Angels*; Howes, *The Sensory Studies Manifesto*, 26–27.

17 Classen, *The Color of Angels*, 5.

18 See, e.g., O. Hardison, *Disappearing Through the Skylight: Culture and Technology in the Twentieth Century* (Penguin, 1990); K. A. Hayles, *How We Became Posthuman* (University of Chicago Press, 1999); A. Plebe & P. Perconti, *The Future of the Artificial Mind* (CRC Press, 2022).

19 Caroline A. Jones (ed.), *Sensorium: Embodied Experience, Technology, and Contemporary Art* (MIT Press, 2006), 5.

20 Ibid., 44.

21 F. Laplantine, *The Life of the Senses: Introduction to a Modal Anthropology*, trans. J. Furniss (Routledge, 2015). We prefer Laplantine's sociological account of the distribution of the sensible to Jacques Rancière's overly philosophical and aestheticized rendition of this notion. Noteworthy analyses in this more sociological vein–that is, accounts that focus on the inclusionary and exclusionary effects of the socio-political distribution of smells and sounds and sights, etc.–include Elisa Fiore, "Navigating Danger Through Nuisance: Racialized Urban Fears, Gentrification, and Sensory Enskilment in Amsterdam," *City and Society* (2023): 1–12; Hsuan Hsu, *The Smell of Risk: Environmental Disparities and Olfactory Aesthetics* (New York University Press, 2020); Rivke Jaffe et al., "What Does Poverty Feel like? Urban Inequality and the Politics of Sensation," *Urban Studies* 57, no. 5 (2020): 1015–31; see also D. Howes, *Sensorial Investigations: A History of the Senses in Anthropology, Psychology, and Law* (Penn State University Press, 2023).

notions as "character," "atmosphere," and "the environmental qualities of a place" – and a plea for thinking of cities "as places for our bodies (and our souls)."[24]

I recall meeting an elderly professor of architecture at the opening of the *Sense of the City* exhibition, who lamented the fact that making scale models out of balsa wood no longer formed part of the architectural curriculum, having been supplanted by computer-assisted design (CAD): "How can you acquire any sense of VOLUME [emphasis his] from a 2-D image on a computer monitor, however 'manipulable' it may be?" He allowed that there were risks to the older pedagogy (e.g., scarred fingers because it takes skill to manipulate an X-acto knife, a skill that many students failed to develop) but, in his estimation, the material benefits far outweigh the costs.

I was brought to a deeper understanding of the implications of my interlocutor's protestation when I met McGill architectural historian Alberto Pérez-Gómez at a subsequent event sponsored by the CCA and read his book *Attunement* (2016). Pérez-Gómez is perhaps the staunchest critic of the digitization of architecture (or architecture that "computes"): "The fact that computers can solve mathematical problems doesn't justify using them as a model for human reasoning; we are neither metal and plastic, nor digital."[25] He posits that the widespread uptake of CAD causes a loss of "the qualitative perception of *places*, the so-called genius loci."[26] According to Pérez-Gómez, the abstraction of the sensible brought on by the proliferating use of computation has precipitated a crisis of sensation, to which he responds by insisting on the importance of the *qualification* of architecture (or, architecture that "makes sense"). In *Attunement*, Pérez-Gómez draws out the sense (or meaning) of such constructs as temperance, character, and analogies to music and poetry or even mathematics (not in the sense of computation but rather the proportionalities of Pythagoras' number harmony). Prior to the Enlightenment, he argues, the construction of buildings was all about creating ambiances deemed to be salubrious, and "producing appropriate atmospheres to the activities they house."[27] Architecture was "mimetic of a traditional cosmos" and, while rooted in place (the *genius loci*), architecture was not static but more a form of "gestural speech" generative of "physiognomic lifeworlds," and most certainly not a "machine for living," in the words of Le Corbusier, grand master of modernist architecture.[28] Pérez-Gómez's advocacy for what could be called "quali(a) tative" research and design methods, where the accent is on qualia not as information or sense data, but as generators of vibrancy and vitality, deserves serious attention.[29]

The year following the *Sense of the City* exhibit, a young architectural historian by the name of David Karmon took up residence as a visiting scholar at the CCA. A passionate student of the senses, Karmon (who is currently chief editor of the *Journal of the Society of Architectural Historians*) recently released *Architecture and the Senses in the Italian Renaissance: The Varieties of Architectural Experience.*[30]

22 M. Zardini (ed.), *Sense of the City: An Alternate Approach to Urbanism* (Canadian Centre for Architecture/Lars Müller, 2005). For an insightful exposé of the lack Zardini alleges to be the case, even within the subfield of eco-urbanism, and some powerful suggestions for how to offset it, see Constance Classen, "Green Pleasures: Sustainable Cities and the Senses," *Harvard Design Magazine* 31 (2009): 66–73.

23 Zardini, *Sense of the City,* 20, 22.

24 As if in response to Zardini's call, perhaps the most rapidly growing field within design art at present is sensory design. See B. Erwine, *Creating Sensory Spaces: The Architecture of the Invisible* (Routledge, 2017), V. Henshaw, K. McLean & D. Medway (eds), *Designing with Smell: Practices, Techniques and Challenges* (Routledge, 2018), E. Lupton & A. Lipps, *The Senses: Design Beyond Vision* (Cooper Hewitt/ Princeton University Press, 2018), C. Spence, *Sensehacking: How to Use the Power of Your Senses for Happier, Healthier Living* (Penguin Viking, 2021), and "Explorations in Sensory Design," https://www.sensorydesign.ca/.

25 A. Pérez-Gómez, *Attunement: Architectural Meaning After the Crisis of Modern Science* (MIT Press, 2016), 157.

26 Ibid., 83.

27 Ibid., 82.

28 Ibid., 74, 170, 171.

29 D. Howes, "Quali(a)tative Methods: Sense-Based Research in the Social Sciences and Humanities," *Qualitative Sociology Review* 18, no. 4 (2022): 26–27, http://www.qualitativesociologyreview.org/ENG/volume63.php.

30 D. Karmon, *Architecture and the Senses in the Italian Renaissance: The Varieties of Architectural Experience* (Cambridge University Press, 2021). Karmon's appointment as chief editor is a sign of how the senses (both as objects of study and means of inquiry) have moved from the margins to the core of architectural history, as they have in history generally (see Martin Jay, "In the Realm of the Senses: An Introduction," *American Historical Review* 116, no. 2 (2011): 307–15).

31 D. Karmon, *Architecture and the Senses in the Italian Renaissance*, 9. Karmon's approach is in line with that of Pérez-Gómez, but he arrived at it independently.

He claims that his book is the first book-length study to address "the early modern built environment in terms of a complex, multisensory immersive experience."[31] With its chapters on "The Building of Devotion" (exemplified by the saturation of the pilgrim's senses in the pavilions that make up the Sacro Monte complex at Varallo), "Sensations of Health and Illness" (as evidenced by the care for the senses of the sick person, and not merely the treatment of disease, in Ospedale Maggiore at Milan and Sacra Infermeria at Valetta), and "Movement in the Built Environment" this book offers a veritable feast for the senses, both individually and *interactively.* Karmon's focus on the interactivity of the senses represents a particularly key breakthrough. By highlighting the phenomenon of "intersensoriality"–"how different senses interact and reinforce each other" (Karmon's definition)–*Architecture and the Senses in the Italian Renaissance* "complicates the process of distinguishing and individuating the specific contributions of the different sensory modes" and, what is more, enucleates how "the senses are deeply intertwined not only among themselves, but also with feeling, emotion, affect, and cognition."[32]

Other scholars have similarly taken up questions of the interrelationship of the senses and the ephemerality of atmospheres. For example, ethnologist Mikkel Bille has focused on atmosphere in such works as *Elements of Architecture: Assembling Archaeology, Atmosphere and the Performance of Building Spaces,* edited with Tim Flohr Sørensen, "Staging Atmospheres," co-edited with Peter Bjerregaard and Sørensen, and, most recently, *The Atmospheric City,* co-authored with Siri Schwabe.[33] Bille advocates for a de-ontological or "elemental" approach to the study of architecture, which shifts the onus from the form of a building to its atmosphere or "ecstasies" and the activities that go on within it. Bille's work is a powerful counterblast to the prevailing temper or headwind of our time, when the "ontological turn" (OT) has resulted in the reification of practically everything–from cultures and worldviews to affective forces or moods to potatoes and mushrooms. The overwhelming focus on "what is" (ontology) in the wake of the OT has obliterated any meaningful attention being paid to epistemology; that is, to such questions as *how* do you know this? what is your approach to *knowing* that which "is"?[34]

Significantly, at the beginning of their introduction to *Elements of Architecture*, Bille and Sørenson cite the example of the Blur Building at Swiss Expo 2002 designed by the firm of Diller, Scofidio and Renfro, approached by way of a jetty into Lake Neuchâtel. Blur was an ephemeral building, devoid of any solidity or form: its façade consisted only of mist, making it the perfect exemplar of Bille and Sørensen's elemental definition of architecture, as well as the late German philosopher Gernot Böhme's theory of the aesthetics of atmospheres, from which they derived much of their inspiration. According to Böhme, atmospheres are like a haze: they are "indeterminate...as regards their ontological status" in that "we are not sure whether we should attribute

32 Ibid., 10. For the original definition of intersensoriality and how it has evolved, see Howes, *Empire of the Senses*, 9–10 and Howes, *The Sensory Studies Manifesto*, 11.

33 M. Bille & T. F. Sørensen, *Elements of Architecture: Assembling Archaeology, Atmosphere and the Performance of Building Spaces* (Routledge, 2016), M. Bille, P. Bjerregaard & T. F. Sørensen, "Staging Atmospheres: Materiality, Culture, and the Texture of the In-Between," *Emotion, Space and Society* 15 (2015): 31–38, M. Bille & S. Schwabe, *The Atmospheric City* (Routledge, 2023).

34 J. Bialecki, "Turn, Turn, Turn," *Public Books* (June 20, 2017), https://www.publicbooks.org/turn-turn-turn/. The problem, however, is with the impact the OT has had on certain branches of philosophy. Regarding the opposition between ontology and what could be called sensology, see Howes, *The Sensory Studies Manifesto,* 34–35, 55–56, 157–58.

35 G. Böhme & J. P. Thibaud, *The Aesthetics of Atmospheres* (Routledge, 2016), 11–12.

36 Ibid.

37 S. Benedito, *Architecture Anatomies: On Design, Weather, and Sensation* (Lars Müller, 2021).

38 Ibid., 17.

39 R. Bendix, "Time of the Senses?" *Current Anthropology* 45, no. 4 (2005): 688–90.

them to the objects or environments from which they proceed or to the subjects who experience them."[35] This is because atmospheres are actually compounded of both, according to Böhme: they are a product of the "co-presence" of subject and object. Specifically, atmospheres are "the *mediums* or the *elements* through which perception, and hence human action and understanding, takes place."[36]

In landscape architecture, this topic has been compellingly addressed by Silvia Benedito, Aga Khan Design Critic in Landscape Architecture at the Harvard Graduate School of Design. In 2016, she organized a symposium at Harvard called "On Atmospheres: Embodiments of Space." Böhme delivered the keynote. Benedito's latest work is entitled *Atmosphere Anatomies: On Design, Weather, and Sensation.* This is a sensational book that will utterly transform your expectations regarding the sensory potentialities latent within landscape architecture.[37]

In the introductory chapter, "The Necessary Paradigm Shift: Space as Atmosphere," Benedito launches her account with this broadside:

> This study begins with two assumptions. The first is that the atmosphere and its meteorological processes are integral to the disciplines of architecture, landscape architecture, and urbanism as spatial practices. The second, closely tied to the first, is that the interdependency of atmospheric processes and their meteorological elements – wind, temperature, sunlight, cloud cover, precipitation, humidity, and atmospheric pressure – is primary to the anatomico-physiological mechanisms and the affiliated sensations for both individual and collective well-being. If one assumes that these assumptions are legitimate and that the making of urban space for the well-being of humankind is central to these design practices, then it is important to strengthen their interdependency in the challenging context of anthropogenic climates.[38]

Subsequent sections in the book include "Atmosphere as Immersive Journey" [on Rousham Garden], "Atmosphere as Program" [on Paley Park] and "Atmosphere as Shared Situation" [on the SESC Pompéia Community Centre].

In the chapter entitled "Chandigarh: On Breathing, Landscape, and Bioclimatic Space" in the "Atmosphere as Thermal Threshold" section of *Atmosphere Anatomies*, Benedito revisits Le Corbusier's work. She brings out how he and his associates were, in actual fact, acutely attuned to local sensescapes and climatic factors and incorporated myriad local sensory cues into their plan for Chandigarh, the new capital city for the states of Punjab and Haryana, India. Among other elements, their plan included creating scope for breathing, spatial transitions between inside and outside [such as "grand empty naves full of shadow, generators of air currents"], walls of greenery, water features, and paradisical retreats. This account challenges those who critique Le Corbusier's oeuvre as ocularcentric and his idea of the architectural form as a machine for living as being the main source of the problem, rather than the solution to the blight of the (non-visual) senses in modern architecture. The implication of Le Corbusier's plan for Chandigarh is that architecture can be conceptualized as a machine for breathing and in service of the thermal regulation of the environment.

This essay has charted the sensorial revolution in the arts and human sciences, which had its roots in the sensuous scholarship proposed by Paul Stoller and has been fleshed out further by Constance Classen, Caroline A. Jones and others. This development in turn set the stage for the emergence of sensorial architecture, urbanism, and landscape design. In closing, I submit that it is high time for those who make the history, theory, and/or practice of architecture their profession to *heed* Zardini and Benedito's call to *awake* from the slumber of reason (Kant), computation, ocularcentrism, and the ontological turn, and to *embrace* the senses–*all of them*. The time of the senses is now.[39]

ERIN PUTALIK + SALLY PUSEDE

SENSE OF SMOG

Erin Putalik is an assistant professor of landscape architecture and architecture at the University of Virginia. She has published widely on building material lifecycle and toxicity considerations, specifically in their relationship to consumption and obsolescence in the built environment. Her current research focuses on how building material toxicity and obsolescence is communicated to design professionals and consumers.

Sally Pusede is an associate professor in the Department of Environmental Sciences at the University of Virginia. Her research combines atmospheric chemistry with environmental justice and public advocacy, an intersection she has written extensively about. She also co-directs the Repair Lab at UVA, which partners UVA researchers and research capacity with local communities to address environmental inequality across Virginia.

+ ENVIRONMENTAL JUSTICE, ENVIRONMENTAL SCIENCE

In April of 1947, Mrs. Betty Williams was pictured in the *Los Angeles Times* wearing a strange contraption. A metal base wrapped her upper torso and rested on her shoulders, supporting a transparent cylinder that fully enclosed her head. Looking like a deep-sea diving helmet or a space suit, both designed for survival in extreme atmospheres, Mrs. Williams's attire was attuned to survival in more everyday environs: the smoggy streets of 1940s Los Angeles.[1] The "smog helmet," an initiative of the Smog Protection Experiment at the University of Southern California, was launched alongside a range of private, state, and federal initiatives aimed at detecting and quantifying, and sometimes controlling, the increasingly noxious air of the city. Despite rapidly developing technology for air composition analysis, Angelinos in the 1940s and '50s knew something was wrong – not from analytical instrumentation; rather, their tearing eyes and aching lungs offered incontrovertible evidence. In fact, the sensing capacity of the human body offered the impetus for public action and resistance in the ensuing two decades, resulting in an unprecedented series of regulations on emissions and, ultimately, California's 1967 Air Quality Act, which itself served as the backbone of the federal Clean Air Act just three years later.

Smog–the word and the experience–infiltrated daily life in Los Angeles in the mid-1940s.[2] When a thick blanket of air pollution enveloped the city in the summer of 1943, burning throats and eyes, it was initially labeled a "gas attack."[3] Just a year and a half after the bombing of Pearl Harbor, and with the United States still embroiled in the Second World War, this reaction both makes sense and relays the sensory intensity of the event.[4] By the end of the summer of 1944, the *LA Times* began referring to this now reoccurring condition as "smog," a portmanteau of smoke and fog. It was not a new term: smog was reportedly coined in 1905 by Henry Antoine des Voeux, physician and officer of London's Coal Smoke Abatement Society, to describe air contamination in Great Britain.[5] In the decade that followed the summer of '44, efforts to understand LA's pollution struggled in this context, as the smog in sunny Los Angeles did not match the black smoke clouds that settled in Northeast US cities and, famously, London during wintertime.[6] The proposed smog-generating suspects quickly expanded, including the impoundment of Lake Mead by the Hoover Dam, chemical plants–particularly those processing butadiene, a petroleum product–trash incineration, and, eventually, small personal housekeeping acts like the shaking of mops and dusters outdoors. Anything, it seemed, was a possible, or at least plausible, cause.

During this period, the capacities of the human senses in smog detection were variously set in service of, or against, a burgeoning set of instrumentation aimed at measuring the components of the polluted air. A half-century prior, in the 1920s, indoor air metrics in the United States had been standardized by the articulated experience of sensing bodies in a recognized experimental setup. An example was the "psychometric room" at the Laboratory of Ventilation and Illumination at the Harvard School of Public Health.[7] In these experiments, the sensing bodies of the human subjects (primarily male engineering students) were placed within the glass boxes of the psychometric rooms and asked to verbally describe their experiences during different activities and under a variety of air temperature and humidity conditions.[8] These sensing bodies were seen as capable of generating meaningful data for the production of the American Society for Heating and Ventilation Engineers' standards.[9]

The glass box of the 1920s psychometric room and the sensorium of its human subjects were focused on thermal comfort, not chemical pollution. Data produced from the senses of certain humans were used to tune the equipment for all other humans' sensory experience of atmospheric "comfort." Three decades later, in 1956, another glass box was leveraged toward different ends in terms of data generation: to provide sensory proof of the health effects of smog in Los Angeles. By this point, the composition and origin of LA's smog had been described by Caltech professor Arie J. Haagen-Smit and colleagues as a chemical reaction of nitrogen oxides and hydrocarbons that were exhausted from Angelinos' beloved cars and sunlight, creating ozone – its primary component.[10] Smit arrived at this research through sensing of a different sort. Smog was affecting vegetation too, observed as "a metallic sheen or glaze" on leaves that was unique to Los Angeles.[11] Residents balked at the idea that individual cars in lieu of large industry could be pinned as a key source and publicly expressed outrage at what seemed, to many, as a ploy to dodge corporate accountability for environmental issues.[12] If the impact of car exhaust on the human body needed to be proven, and the proof needed to be sensory and public, a glass smog chamber could be just the thing.

S. Smith Griswold, a "blond, buff, specimen" and head of Los Angeles's Air Pollution Control District, volunteered his sensing body for the production of the right kind of evidence.[13] Conflating spectacle and experiment, Griswold sat in the chamber, surrounded by Los Angeles press, for two hours while it was filled with the chemical components of LA's smog: nitrogen oxides, hydrocarbons, and soon, ozone. Griswold emerged from the chamber, his eyes tearing, head aching, finding concentration difficult, and with diminished lung capacity and altered sense of taste, his body's response providing public, and publicly performed, evidence of the health effects of the smog.[14] Griswold's smog chamber demonstration, while not conducted under experimental conditions that were satisfactory to doctors interviewed afterward, was a conspicuous spectacle that was executed in precisely the parlance of smog detection that had been most convincing to the citizens of Los Angeles: the way that the bodily comfort and senses were impacted, relayed anecdotally, in first-person, and with clear references to understood daily experiences. After all, Griswold summarized the aggregate effects of the smog chamber in what feels like a quintessentially mid-century manner, as "something like having two martinis before dinner."[15]

This mode of evidence production worked because of how the smog problem had been articulated since its emergence. It was defined from the outset by the residents of Los Angeles in terms of their senses. Take, for example, Astronomer John Hickox peering over LA from the Mount Wilson Observatory in 1944, who described the diminishing visibility, saying, "We used to be able to see Mt. San Jacinto, Palomar and all the way to Point Loma. Now sometimes we can't even see Old Baldy from here."[16] The missing landscapes, reported in terms of the city's visual memory, were complemented and reinforced by an emerging slew of photographs—becoming almost a genre unto itself—of the smog-obscured city. These bright, hazy landscapes were captured by the camera and caused by small particles in the air, particles that were chemically produced in the atmosphere alongside ozone that scattered sunlight like clouds. Eyes offered another kind of evidence as well: one of the most sensitive elements in the body and protected only by a very thin membrane, the human cornea readily registers the presence of air pollutants, including those in the air of Los Angeles, such as the potent lachrymator, peroxy acetyl nitrate. Citizens "mopping watering eyes" were pictured in news media walking through smoggy scenes, a visualization of the environmental catastrophe and its human effects.[17]

It was not just the eyes; lungs burned too, and nasal passages. The act of breathing was a reminder of the severity of the issue. In 1944, the Altadena Property Owners League began regularly protesting the effects of the fumes on their quality of life. When the District Attorney's office conveyed to the League that their perception of the smog's effects was most likely psychological, the League's secretary shot back that the DA should come over to Altadena to get some "lungs full of psychology."[18] Breathing was believing – a sensory experience serving as the impetus and evidence for public action and resistance.[19]

During this time, technological advancements in observing air composition, such as the "smog catcher" of 1945, were producing another kind of evidence. Adapted from a device that had been used in the Division of Industrial Hygiene of LA's Health Department to protect worker health, the smog catcher measured particles electrostatically precipitated out of the air.[20] This tool was for use by technical experts, and, in its first day of operation, Captain Thomas Marsh of the US Public Health Service reported the smog catcher detected a factor of two higher particle concentrations in the air than would cause irritation (and, therefore, could be sensed by bodies). However, while the smog catcher quantified the amount of particles in the air, at times, it was also used to assure residents that their concerns were nothing more than the "clean, cool mist" of fog.[21] The evidence generated by the "smog catcher" and ensuing sensors was thus positioned as capable of overriding Angelinos' own sensory experiences, transferring authority from embodied experiences to mechanical devices, which could sense, as the "smog catcher" did, in authoritative terms such as milligrams of pollutant per cubic meter of air. At the same time, these early devices were often rhetorically imbued with the same capacities wielded by the public in their own claims of smog's effects. A 1946 instrument developed in part by the Air Pollution Control Board was described in the *LA Times* as being adept at "SMOG 'SMELLING'" and "Smog-Hunter" airplanes became olfactory proxies that generated concrete numbers of the concentrations of smog components for the city's technocrats and regional scientists.

Sight, linked initially to human memories of once visible landmarks, also underwent a standardization process during this period for quantifying the sources of smog. The Ringelmann Chart was one such way, explored by the Air Pollution Control Board alongside the smog sniffers in the mid-1940s.[22] Meant as a tool to measure the density of smoke emissions from industrial facilities, the chart was developed in recently industrialized Paris in the mid-19th century. In lieu of relying on shades of gray, which might vary due to different ink densities

1 "Smog Helmet," *Los Angeles Times* (April 16, 1947), 1:7.

2 It has been noted that visibility in and around Los Angeles began to decline in 1939, with "intervals of smoky air" occurring in 1940 and 1941. Thus, the "gas attack" of 1943 was not the first of its kind, but was more widespread, intense, and visible than previous episodes. See Benjamin Ross & Steven Amter, *The Polluters: The Making of Our Chemically Altered Environment* (Oxford University Press, 2010), 75.

3 "City Hunting for Source of 'Gas Attack'," *Los Angeles Times* (July 27, 1943), 1. See also: California Air Resources Board, "History," https://ww2.arb.ca.gov/about/history (accessed November 2, 2023).

4 Numerous articles in the *Los Angeles Times* in the year prior to the smog event instructed Angelinos what to do in case of a gas attack and reported on alleged Japanese gas attacks elsewhere in the world.

5 Peter Brimblecombe, "Deciphering the Chemistry of Los Angeles Smog, 1945–1995," in James Rodger Fleming & Ann Johnson (eds), *Toxic Airs: Body, Place, Planet in Historical Perspective* (University of Pittsburgh Press, 2014), 96; Ross & Amter, *The Polluters*, 73–75.

6 Anne Whiston Spirn explored LA Smog and its lived effects in the chapter "Dirt and Discomfort" in her book *The Granite Garden: Urban Nature and Human Design* (Basic Books, 1984), 41–61.

7 For further reading on the evolution of the psychometric chart and other psychometric rooms, see Wulf Böer, "Synthetic Air," *Future Anterior* 13, no. 2 (Winter 2016): 77–101. Böer also describes early attempts to quantify the smelliness of the air using the 19th-century "odorometer."

8 Michelle Murphy, *Sick Building Syndrome and the Problem of Uncertainty: Environmental Exposure, Technoscience, and Women Workers* (Duke University Press, 2006).

9 Ibid., 19–34. As Murphy observes, the EPA did not study indoor air pollution in a concerted way until it was congressionally mandated in 1984. Ibid, 82.

10 California Air Resources Board, "Dr. Arie Haagen-Smit," https://ww2.arb.ca.gov/about/leadership/dr-arie-haagen-smit# (accessed Nov 12, 2023). Haagen-Smit was the Founding Chairman of the California Air Resources Board.

11 A. J. Haagen-Smit, et al., "Investigation on Injury to Plants from Air Pollution in the Los Angeles Area," *Plant Physiology* 27, no. 1 (January 1952): 18–34.

12 Roger Turner, "Smith Griswold Sells the War Against Smog," *Distillations Magazine: A Journal of the Science History Institute* (October 1, 2019), https://sciencehistory.org/stories/magazine/smith-griswold-sells-the-war-against-smog/.

13 "You've Got Troubles? Shed Tear for Smog Control Chief," *The Virginian-Pilot* (September 30, 1956), 13.

14 Ibid. *The Virginian-Pilot* also stated that while Griswold was exposed to 2 ppm of ozone, the highest recorded level in Los Angeles at that time was 0.9 ppm, and that a smog alert goes into effect after 0.5 ppm. See also Turner, "Smith-Griswold Sells."

15 Ibid. ("You've got Troubles?"); An editorial a few years later described the experience of inhaling ozone as making "you feel kinda giddy, like the third Martini." See Dick Hyland, "The Hyland Fling," *Los Angeles Times* (April 8, 1948), 34.

16 Ray Zeman, "City 'Smog' Laid to Dozen Causes: Autos, Chemical Plants, Sewers All Contribute, Experts Report," *Los Angeles Times* (Sept 18, 1944), 13.

17 "Smog Again Holds Sway; Mercury 91," *Los Angeles Times* (September 13, 1945), 1.

18 "Atmospheric Freak Holds 'Smog' Over City," *Los Angeles Times* (September 24, 1944), 19.

19 For more on the role of smell as environmental authority in New York and Chicago in the 19th century, see "Smelling Committees and Authority over City Air," in Melanie K. Kiechle, *Smell Detectives: An Olfactory History of Nineteenth-Century Urban America* (University of Washington Press, 2019), 138–69.

20 "Fumes Check Under Way," *Los Angeles Times* (September 14, 1945), 13.

21 Ibid.

22 Ed Ainsworth, "County Smog-Fighting Staff Traces Evil Fumes' Sources," *Los Angeles Times* (October, 18, 1946), 9, https://latimes.newspapers.com/article/the-los-angeles-times-county-smog-fight/103936284/.

23 U.S. Department of the Interior, Bureau of Mines, "Ringelmann Smoke Chart," *Information Circular* 8333 (1967). https://www.cdc.gov/niosh/mining/userfiles/works/pdfs/ic8333.pdf.

24 Ed Ainsworth, "County Smog-Fighting Staff Traces Evil Fumes' Sources." Ultimately, the Ringelmann Chart was used to hold polluters accountable and was incorporated into the state Health and Safety Code (Section 242420).

25 Zeman "City 'Smog' Laid to Dozen Causes," 13.

26 "New Code Adopted for Smog Forecast," *Los Angeles Times* (September 22, 1955), 1. In 1956, the smog green/smog red coding was replaced out of concern it evoked images of green and red clouds settling over LA in the minds of people outside the city. Los Angeles Councilman Charles Navarro, "In the East I'm told they think we have two kinds of smog – one red and one green."

and absorptions and/or ink substrates, the Ringelmann Chart used black lines of different spacing and thicknesses, creating four steps of effective grayscale.[23] Over the following decade, the chart was used as a companion to the eyes when concrete evidence of unchecked smoke pollution was needed to halt air polluters within the city, with this standardization enabling a higher degree of enforcement.[24] Seeing might be believing, but standardized sight, facilitated by ink-density comparison charts, conferred reproducibility, credibility, and enforceability.

Despite the personal nature of embodied sensing, smog concerns in Los Angeles were often articulated with a democratizing illusion and largely pursued along those lines. An early report from the County Fumes and Smoke Commission described the environmental condition of the city, ringed with mountains to create a single "room," as such: "A community of more than 2,000,000 people is shut up in a vast room with doors and windows closed" and subjected to "a hellish cloud that fills the room and is indifferent to municipal boundaries."[25] The topographic bowl of the city became, in the early days of LA smog awareness, a common space with urban occupants who shared a collective purpose and fate. By 1955, that fate was printed daily in the newspaper: "SMOG GREEN: No emergency expected," but "SMOG RED: Heavy smog forecast (your help needed)." Officials proclaimed, "smog is a community problem," with the colorful codes doubling as a call to action for "civic-minded" Angelenos to do their part, for example, by limiting their personal driving.[26] Air's unbounded mobility, in this imaginary, was a great equalizer, holding the potential to spur collective action across the varied geography of the city.

In the more than half-century since LA was described as a great room holding those with a common fate, the unequal distribution and impacts of air pollution have been shown again and again.[27] As vehicles emit nitrogen oxides and hydrocarbons that produce ozone and particles, how close one lives to heavily trafficked roadways has its own air pollution-related health consequences.[28] When those roadways became freeways in the 1950s–'70s, officials disproportionately routed them through the neighborhoods of Black, Latinx, Asian, and poor Angelinos, displacing residents and worsening air quality locally for those who remained.[29]

Since 1970, ozone regulations, including controls on vehicles, have reduced LA's smog to levels such that they less affect the immediate senses of large portions of the population.[30] However, for those living near pollution sources and members of sensitive groups, such as people with asthma, smog in Los Angeles continues to register as physical discomfort. With the Clean Air Act focused on concentration-based National Ambient Air Quality Standards (NAAQS), mechanical sensing evidence, and only from designated instrumentation, became the ultimate authority on the severity of smog.[31] As embodied sensing—and the forms of community advocacy it once facilitated—have been sidelined, the absence of data from sensing machines produces, in a way, a denial of the existence of air pollution and the harm it causes. In response, a new mode of personal, mechanical sensing has become popular – small, lower-cost devices for non-technical experts that monitor the concentrations of smog components.[32] These devices detect pollution levels we may not feel, but they are most common in locations where both the experience of air quality continues to be an embodied one and sensing instrumentation for NAAQS compliance is absent. Still, measurements from these devices bureaucratically lack the epistemic value of NAAQS-approved analytical instruments, with the physical realities of air pollution's severity ultimately determined by officials and technical experts through the specific evidence created by designated forms of mechanical sensing.

This episode of Los Angeles history, in which the articulation of human sensory experience developed alongside mechanical sensing capacity, scientific research on the components of the smog, and standards and mandates controlling its production, shows us how important the relationship of embodied and technological sensing is in the articulation of emergent environmental and health issues. The authority of physical discomfort, sight and remembered views, and smell were all registered heartily in the public discourse surrounding early smog detection. The sensory experience of smog was both verified and eventually superseded by the sensing equipment that evolved alongside the health and environmental challenges it opposed. Between the first "gas attack" of 1943 and S. Smith Griswold's glass smog chamber experiment/spectacle of 1957, the components of urban smog and their effects on the human body relied explicitly on personal reports and scientific observations alike. As access to air quality sensors opens, a new democratizing illusion—one of limitless data from personal and distributed sensors—risks occluding the human impacts of unequal access to the decision-making authority that the analytical instrumentation reinforces. The 1947 image of Betty Williams in her smog helmet, wearing an individual high-tech device that masked her own senses to confer a degree of (experimental) safety, turns out to have been strangely prescient, sidelining her own embodied experience to rely on technology for protection. We would do well to remember the messy, ambivalent, and imbricated history of early air quality sensory evidence in Los Angeles to continue to make space for the embodied, anecdotal, and personal in advocating for and advancing concerns around air quality.

27 Jason G. Su, et al. "An Index for Assessing Demographic Inequalities in Cumulative Environmental Hazards with Application to Los Angeles, California," *Environmental Science & Technology* 43, no. 20 (2009): 7626–34; Julian D. Marshall, "Environmental inequality: Air Pollution Exposures in California's South Coast Air Basin" *Atmospheric Environment* 42, no. 21 (July 2008): 5499–503.

28 Mary Angelique G. Demetillo, et al., "Space-Based Observational Constraints on NO2 Air Pollution Inequality From Diesel Traffic in Major US Cities," *Geophysical Research Letters* 48, no. 17 (2021); Jaiqi Shen, et al., "Aerosol Oxidative Potential in the Greater Los Angeles Area: Source Apportionment and Associations with Socioeconomic Position," *Environmental Science & Technology* 56, no. 24 (2022): 17795–804; Lisa Schweitzer, "Environmental Justice and Hazmat Transport: A Spatial Analysis in Southern California," *Transportation Research Part D: Transport and Environment* 11, no. 6 (November 2006): 408–21.

29 Anastasia Loukaitou-Sideris, "The Implications of Freeway Siting in California: Four Case Studies on the Effects of Freeways on Neighborhoods of Color," UCLA Institute of Transportation Studies/ Research Report from the Pacific Southwest Region University Transportation Center (2023); Geoff Boeing, Yougeng Lu & Clemens Pilgram, "Local Inequities in the Relative Production of and Exposure to Vehicular Air Pollution in Los Angeles," *Urban Studies* 60, no. 12 (2023): 2351–68; John Molitor, et al., "Identifying Vulnerable Populations through an Examination of the Association Between Multipollutant Profiles and Poverty," *Environmental Science & Technology* 45, no. 18 (2011): 7754–60.

30 D. D. Parrish & W. R. Stockwell, "Urbanization and Air Pollution: Then and Now," *Eos* 96, https://eos.org/features/urbanization-air-pollution-now; Ilana B. Pollack, et al., "Trends in Ozone, Its Precursors, and Related Secondary Oxidation Products in Los Angeles, California: A Synthesis of Measurements from 1960 to 2010," *Journal of Geophysical Research: Atmospheres* 118, no. 11 (2013): 5893–911.

31 J. Gilliam & E. Hall, "Reference and Equivalent Methods Used to Measure National Ambient Air Quality Standards (NAAQS) Criteria Air Pollutants - Volume I," U.S. Environmental Protection Agency, Washington, DC, EPA/600/R-16/139 (2016).

32 PurpleAir, https://map.purpleair.com/.

VR

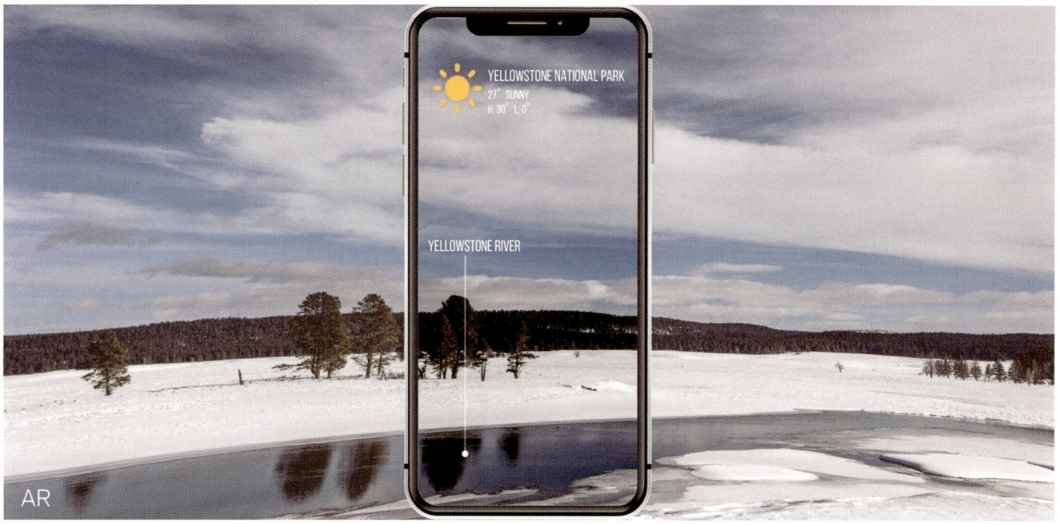
YELLOWSTONE NATIONAL PARK
YELLOWSTONE RIVER
AR

MR

CHRIS SALTER

SENSORIMOTOR ACTS

Chris Salter is professor and director of the Immersive Arts Space at the Zürich University of the Arts (ZHdK) and Professor Emeritus of Computation Arts at Concordia University, Montréal. His artistic work has been seen internationally at such venues as the Venice Architecture Biennale, Barbican Centre, Berliner Festspiele, Wiener Festwochen, and Grand Palais Immersif, among many others. He is the author of *Entangled* (2010), *Alien Agency* (2015), and *Sensing Machines* (2022), all published by MIT Press.

+ SPATIAL COMPUTING

On June 5, 2023, Apple, one of a handful of US-based tech companies with more than a trillion-dollar market capitalization, pretended to glance into the future. On a stage inside Sir Norman Foster's UFO-esque headquarters for the company in the Silicon Valley enclave of Cupertino, Apple CEO Tim Cook announced the company's latest offering: a 2kg headset called Vision Pro. In almost hyperbolic terms, Cook matter-of-factly stated that Apple was offering not only a device, but also a new technological paradigm: one he called *spatial computing*.

For anyone working in computer science, computer graphics, game design, or architecture, Apple's revisionist history gives room for pause. When Cook made his announcement, the term "spatial computing" was already in widespread use, not only in research circles, but also in industry. Originally appearing in the work of an MIT Media Lab master's student in the early 2000s but only utilized in consumer devices about 20 years later, spatial computing was originally defined as the ability of computers to "retain and manipulate referents to real bodies, objects, and spaces."[1] For example, the promotion for the Magic Leap headset, a wearable "augmented reality" device that was released in 2018 to much hype, only to crater out commercially less than a year after its debut, argued that while VR is almost perniciously depicted as "digital environments that shut out the real world" and AR describes "digital content on top of your real world," spatial computing describes "digital content that interacts with your real world and you."[2]

A recent scientific paper defines spatial computing across two scales. The first claims that spatial computing involves a macro description of technologies that allow us to grasp an "emerging immersive global data ecosystem." Yet, in the same article, another argument appears – one that aims to situate spatial computing not as an abstracted information system out in server clouds, but as a situated, spatially oriented technology focused on "bodily awareness and self-presence."[3]

The concept that spatial computing involves "localized" and "embodied" characteristics is not particularly novel. Such a paradigm was described many decades earlier in a more prosaic location: a NYC conference room filled with engineers attending the even more prosaically named "International Federation for Information Processing Conference." Ivan Sutherland, an MIT PhD engineer, offered up his version of the future in a 20-minute talk and, later, a short paper titled "The Ultimate Display." In it, he sketched out a vision in which computing would begin not only to find its way into the physical environment, but also to radically transform how we would perceive that environment through mathematics and electronics.[4] Indeed, in his essay, Sutherland sketched out an almost science-fiction sounding vision of computing – one in which the relationship between mathematical and material reality was hybridized.

Sutherland's speculations were not to remain the stuff of concept. In 1968, he sought to make them a material reality. Starting at Harvard, Sutherland, together with his PhD student Robert Sproul, developed what became known as the first three-dimensional head mounted display (HMD) – a device that aimed "to surround the user with displayed three-dimensional information" based on the movement of their heads.[5] A marvel of compact electronics, the display, built in a basement laboratory at Harvard, consisted of an eyeglasses-like headset outfitted with two cathode ray tubes (the same used in televisions, albeit at a miniature scale) in place of the eyes and connected to a suspended counterbalanced robotic arm loaded with ultrasonic sensors that could track the head movement of the user so that the image in the display would continually update. This augmented vision system generated binocular imagery so that the image appeared to float in mid-air and changed perspective as the wearer moved around. Although Sutherland did not use the term virtual reality, what was dubbed the Sword of Damocles (due to its two-ton weight, which precipitously hung over the user's head) is now seen as the technological precursor to all the two-letter acronyms that describe these new mixes of the physical and the computational world: VR, AR, and MR (mixed reality).

Unlike contemporary visions of virtual worlds, like the so-called metaverse, Sutherland's inspiration was not derived from science fiction. It came from military research – namely, the military defense contractor Bell Helicopter, which, at that time, was exploring how to land helicopters in the dark. Rigging an infrared camera under the helicopter whose viewpoint could be remotely accessed, the motor-controlled camera could be repositioned by a pilot's head movement while the pilot's field of view matched that of the camera itself. Bell's telepresence night vision system, already developed in 1963, was thus an appropriate technology to assist the US Military in fighting a war in the darkened jungles of Vietnam.

The Bell Helicopter HMD could be used to sense an environment that lay physically beyond the immediate human senses. Yet, Sutherland aimed to improve on Bell's device with his Harvard-created HMD by moving to the next step. As opposed to a camera, he felt that a computer could better do the job, but since none were powerful enough to do so at that time, his team had to build its own equipment.[6] Indeed, such a move foreshadows what would later be understood as a new approach to computing in which perception, action, and physical space would be coupled with and augmented by computation. In this way, spatial computing seems to be the long-in-development breakthrough to conceive a new way of thinking about the relationship of computers in the world: one that aims to take the natural-human-environment mix into account while allowing the computer itself to vanish into the background. Computing was not only envisioned to be in the environment – *it would become it*.

The fact that HMD-enabled spatial computing was and still is linked to military technology should come as no surprise. After all, Advanced Research Projects Association (ARPA) and the Office of Naval Research funded Sutherland's Harvard research on the HMD. Such imagined military applications that combined computationally generated and real environments operating through and on the body and its sensing possibilities would continue to multiply. For example, Ana Viseau and Lucy Suchman's work on body augmentation through so-called "wearable computing," especially in the context of military applications, argues that worn technologies such as the HMD provide "full-spectrum dominance through the achievement of information superiority."[7] In using wearable technologies, "The augmented soldier is seen as a fully integrated information network, the central issue being to establish a balance between visibility and invisibility, access and control in military operations."[8]

What is key here is the line between visibility and invisibility that can be situated in a nexus that links the human body to wearable computing. While wearable computing has long been thought of as technologies that both process data and are attached to the body, Viseau and Suchman describe how such technologies, which are argued (by their manufacturers) to be "aware" and "sentient," are so due to sensors such as accelerometers or temperature devices. Thus, a wearable device like the HMD rigged with such sensing and computational possibilities enables "information technology...to extend the body into the environment" itself.[9]

The extension and augmentation of the human senses to make sense of or, in the case of military simulation, to intervene in the environment has long shaped 20th-century imaginaries of computing technologies in their quest to become increasingly invisible. Indeed, in a quote that demonstrates the shift in thinking of computers as objects to computers as malleable systems designed to reshape our conception of spaces around and beyond our body and senses seamlessly, MIT Media Lab founder Nicholas Negroponte famously stated:

> Computing is not about computers anymore. It is about living. The giant central computer, the so-called mainframe, has been almost universally replaced by personal computers. We have seen computers move out of giant air-conditioned rooms into closets, then onto desktops, and now into our laps and pockets. But this is not the end.[10]

Negroponte also did not invent this idea that the computer would eventually transition from the mainframe server room to the human body and beyond. Such a concept was set off in the late 1980s in Silicon Valley under the research program of ubicomp (ubiquitous computing) when American computer scientist Marc Weiser proposed such a model as part of a larger research program at the Xerox corporation's Palo-Alto-based research lab – better known by its acronym of Xerox PARC. PARC defined ubicomp as a "new field of computer science, one that speculated on a physical world richly and invisibly interwoven with sensors, actuators, displays, and computational elements, embedded seamlessly in the everyday objects of our lives and connected through a continuous network."[11] The ubicomp vision sought by Weiser, Rich Gold, and other researchers at the PARC computer science lab was to embed computing back into the lived environment; to focus on how computation could help to mediate and even augment human-to-human interaction in contrast to forcing users to interact directly with computers (so-called human-computer interaction, or HCI).

While PARC developed a range of technologies as part of the ubicomp program, ranging from remote "tabs" that could wirelessly communicate with large wall-size displays, to a book-sized electronic pad, perhaps the most important articulation of this concept was an article that Weiser wrote for *Scientific American* in 1991 in which he laid out some key ideas of the ubiquity of computing. The core idea that Weiser announced was the disappearance of computing technology with the almost prophetic statement that "The most profound technologies are those that disappear. They weave themselves into the fabric of everyday life until they are indistinguishable from it."[12] In other words, ubicomp was not just about reducing the size of computers from ugly beige or black boxes sitting under workers' desks. It was about conceiving a new way of thinking about computers in the world, one that takes into account the natural human environment and allows the computers themselves to vanish into what researchers call the background – that is, *the periphery of our attention.*

Despite Apple, Meta, and HTC's continued attempts to create an HMD that looks like a pair of fashionable Uvex ski goggles while simultaneously functioning as a computing device, the bulkiness of such worn machines seems a far cry from Weiser's vision of computing vanishing into the background. Indeed, he says as much when he argues that ubicomp is "profoundly different from VR," which attempts to create a computational representation of the world in the computer.[13] Instead, ubiquitous computing is a kind of "embodied virtuality" that refers to the process of drawing computers out of their electronic shells. The virtuality of the computer involves the different ways in which it can be altered, processed, and analyzed – in other words, *how the computer is brought into the physical world.*

Bringing computing into a new relationship with the physical world is indeed what ubicomp is about. In this context, Weiser argued that computers would increasingly develop new kinds of understandings and awareness of the real world such as where the machine is spatially located, how it links up with other computers, and how it adapts to the world. As Weiser argued, "If a computer knows merely what room it is in, it can adapt its behavior in significant ways without requiring even a hint of artificial intelligence."[14] Here, Weiser is not referring to what we commonly understand today by the term artificial intelligence–deep-learning-based neural networks that run generative models that take existing data sets and statistically rearrange them, such as the case with GPT, Stable Diffusion, or Sora–systems that not inconsequently have a far greater impact on the natural environment than deploying hardware-based sensor networks (which often run on low-power algorithms to sustain their energy over months of use). Instead, like a genealogy of researchers before him, such as the philosopher Hubert Dreyfus, the linguist George Lakoff, or even the early AI pioneer Terry Winograd, Weiser was out to critique the concept of intelligent systems as solely symbolic, logic-driven entities that would attempt to uncover the deep "rules" of what constitutes human behavior to *simulate* the world inside a logical machine.

Upon closer examination of Weiser's arguments, we get a sense that he was proposing not only a technological revolution, but also a *social*-technical one – a new model of interaction among people. Of course, Weiser was not naïve. He acknowledged there would be problems with this approach, one of which is privacy. Yet, at the same time, the "naturalization" of computing, of taking the natural human environment into account, suggested a powerful idea: that interaction with machines is not only through writing or language, but also through our very different culturally shaped bodies acting as interfaces with the physical world. What psychologists call embodied or sensorimotor interactions involving the sensory and motor parts of the body are second nature. We do not think for a moment about how we walk, if we are nondisabled that is. We just do it. Even those with reduced motion interact expressively with the world, using their eyes, fingers, or other parts of their bodies. Some engineers felt that computing should follow suit.[15]

In other words, the key concept in ubicomp, and with that spatial computing, is putting the human body and the environment it inhabits at the center of an information network: bodies as literal interfaces between the machine and the environment. By now, it should be obvious that HMDs used in VR and increasingly in AR are not simply an extension but, as the psychoacoustician and ARPA manager J. C. R. Licklider called it, a creator of a "symbiotic relationship between a man [person] and a fast information retrieval and data processing machine."[16] This emphasis on the primacy of the sensorimotor body is what researchers term a "technology interface" for embodied action and, thus, characterizes spatial computing technology in relationship to the HMD as a "perceptual technology" – a technology that models human perceptual mechanisms and traits.[17] In other words, we can see there is also a strong claim that extended reality (XR) is a clear example of what computing science has termed "embodied interaction" – interaction that involves the reality of experience through an interplay between embodied perception and action and symbolic structure of machines and the environment in which such action takes place.[18]

The concept of embodied interaction seems to liberate the human body chained to a desk and interacting with a world through a screen from the formidable constraints of computing. Such a vision of freedom of movement and expression has also recently materialized in Apple's new universe of spatial computing. In fact, as of winter 2024, the latest YouTube and TikTok memes feature channels filled with self-anointed early adopters wearing their newly acquired Apple Vision Pros (at least those who could afford a 3,500+ USD piece of technology) gleefully walking around in streets, waving their hands in the air, gesticulating wildly and appearing to summon spirits out of thin air. But when we speak of the body as an interface, exactly what kinds of bodies are we looking at in these videos? Clearly, not bodies that do not have the luxury of interacting with their physical surroundings in such a carefree way because of using a wheelchair, having to carry tanks of oxygen, or simply not being able to raise their arms or hands. Indeed, the "intensified corporeal sensations" that media scholar Anna Munster claims have long been promised by XR do not apply to all bodies or even environments.[19] In fact, it might be considered hazardous or fatal for even abled bodies in harsh environments to walk around the streets of Bangalore or even Rome wearing the Vision Pro, as one's peripheral vision, even when turning the device's "reality dial" to open up the virtual space to the real space, is limited.

Such non-normative bodies could help us to conjure up other imaginaries for spatial computing – ones that transcend the standard fantasy of jumping in a game and flying through physical space by way of computation that is the stuff of Silicon Valley fantasies. What happens when the sensorimotor system is impaired? When one cannot begin to imagine walking, let alone intricately manipulating hand controllers to navigate inside a 3D-generated world? One idea in development is to utilize other parts of the body, for example, the mouth and the tongue, that have traditionally been ignored by technologists as sites for body-based interfaces to navigate inside virtual spaces.[20] Another direction is to hack the software, giving disabled users the ability to "amplify" or "scale" their own gestures. By moving a slider or parameter, much like DJs or electronic musicians who use their own gestures to generate or manipulate sound, disabled users could directly be given control over these worn devices, scaling their own actions and thus, being given influence over the black box interfaces of these technologies. In this instance, instead of thinking about how bodies adapt to technologies, we can then ask what it would mean to take the affordances of different bodies interacting in specific environments as a catalyst for a new way of thinking about spatial computing – one in which computation adapts and transforms itself based on the multiplicity and situatedness of bodies and spaces that interact with it rather than the other way around. In this sense, the vision that Ivan Sutherland posed more than six decades ago, to think of the "ultimate display" as a "kinesthetic display" in a room where such a technology could control the very "existence of matter," could then be fulfilled, albeit in an unexpected way.[21] Perhaps matter might not be changed, but the imaginaries of human-to-environment interaction would certainly be.

1 S. Greenwold, "Spatial Computing," Massachusetts Institute of Technology, Master's Thesis (2003), https://acg.media.mit.edu/people/simong/transfers/layout.pdf, 9.

2 Magic Leap Developer, "Magic Leap," https://ml1-developer.magicleap.com/ja-jp/learn/guides/design-why-magic-leap (accessed February 29, 2024).

3 G. Yenduri, et al. "Spatial Computing: Concept, Applications, Challenges and Future Directions," *arXiv* (2024), https://arxiv.org/abs/2402.07912, 2.

4 Ivan E. Sutherland, "The Ultimate Display," in *Proceedings of the IFIP Congress* 2 (1965): 506–08.

5 Ivan E. Sutherland, "A Head-Mounted Three Dimensional Display," in *Proceedings of the December 9–11, 1968 Joint Computer Conference*, Part I (1968), 757.

6 V. R. Shop, "Bell System HMD," https://www.virtual-reality-shop.co.uk/bell-system-hmd-1963/ (accessed February 24, 2024).

7 A. Viseu & L. Suchman, "Wearable Augmentations: Imaginaries of the Informed Body," in J. Edwards, P. Harvey & P. Wade (eds), *Technologized Images, Technologized Bodies* (Berghahn Books, 2010), 166.

8 Ibid.

9 Ibid, 162.

10 N. Negroponte, *Being Digital* (Hodder and Stoughton, 1995), 65-67.

11 M. Weiser, R. Gold & J. S. Brown, "The Origins of Ubiquitous Computing Research at PARC in the Late 1980s," *IBM Systems Journal* 38, no. 4 (1999): 694.

12 M. Weiser, "The Computer for the 21st Century," *Scientific American* 265, no. 3 (1991): 94.

13 Ibid.

14 Ibid., 98.

15 C. Salter, *Sensing Machines: How Sensors Shape Our Everyday Life* (MIT Press, 2022).

16 J. C. R. Licklider, "Man-Computer Symbiosis," *IRE Transactions on Human Factors in Electronics* HFE-1, no. 1 (1960): 6.

17 H. Rheingold, *Virtual Reality: Exploring the Brave New Technologies* (Simon and Schuster, 1991).

18 P. Dourish, *Where the Action Is: The Foundations of Embodied Interaction* (MIT Press, 2001); J. M. Flach & J. G. Holden, "The Reality of Experience: Gibson's Way," *Presence Teleoperators & Virtual Environments* 7, no. 1 (1998): 90–95.

19 A. Munster, *Materializing New Media: Embodiment in Information Aesthetics* (Dartmouth College Press, 2006), 91.

20 P. Jain, "Crip Sensorama," https://ars.electronica.art/university/de/crip-sensorama/ (accessed April 14, 2024).

21 Sutherland, "The Ultimate Display," 507.

ALEXA VAUGHN

DEAF EXPERIENCE: BEYOND ADA STANDARDS

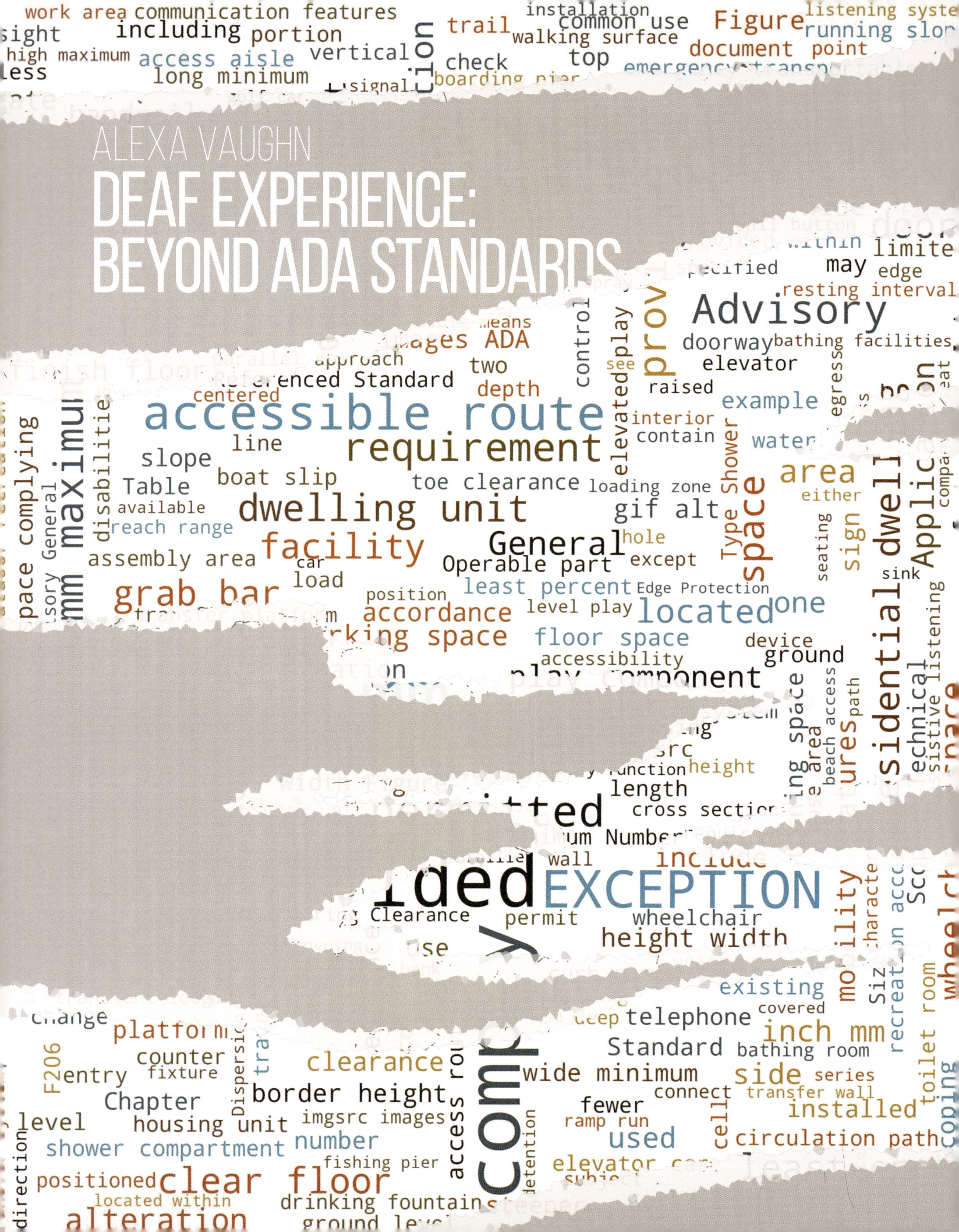

Alexa Vaughn is a Deaf landscape designer, accessibility specialist, and PhD student in Architecture + Urban Design at UCLA. She is an expert in designing for the Deaf community, facilitating disabled community engagement, and applying the ADA and Universal Design to landscape architecture. She has been featured in numerous publications, and much of her work can be found at www.designwithdisabledpeoplenow.com. Vaughn is a Fellow of the American Academy in Rome.

+ DESIGN, DISABILITY STUDIES

I live a life between the hearing and Deaf worlds. I have been deaf since the age of eight but did not begin to identify as culturally Deaf until the age of 23, when I was finally exposed to Deaf culture and began learning American Sign Language (ASL). It was not until I was 23 that I realized it was my birthright to claim this part of myself that I had long been told needed to be "fixed" and, as a result, had hidden from the world. Because I had acquired my deafness post-linguistically, it began as a sense of "hearing loss" but later transformed into "a state of being in all its complexity," known as "Deaf Gain."[1] This early sense of loss and not-belonging was a direct consequence of the dominant medical model worldview, which is eugenics-centric and treats disabled people as a problem to be "cured," rather than following a social model worldview, which considers the built environment and society at large as in need of radical transformation.[2]

At the heart of my disability is my inability to participate seamlessly in the dominant mode of auditory communication, which isolates me in the public and private spheres. Because my everyday world is predominantly rooted in auditory rather than visual language–and the public landscape is designed to facilitate the former–I often feel like a fish out of water in the built environment. There is an ableist assumption that language is spoken and heard, not visually read or signed. As a Deaf person and a woman, I am often on edge in public, compensating with my eyesight while also feeling as if I must somehow amplify and fully attune to the one sense that my body cannot provide.

Helen Keller (1880–1968), historically the most famous DeafBlind person, remarked that "to be cut off from hearing is to be isolated."[3] Keller's statement is correct: I too often feel sensory isolation in a hearing world and in the absence of Deaf community. Keller lived at a time when eugenics was rampant. Regardless of the ideologies of her time, she was a radical activist: a socialist, a suffragist, a co-founder of the American Civil Liberties Union (ACLU), a staunch anti-racist, a supporter of the National Association for the Advancement of Colored People (NAACP), a celebrated orator, and the author of 14 books.[4] Yet despite her overwhelmingly accomplished and meaningful life, she still held views of internalized ableism toward herself and other disabled people. Until her death, her greatest regret was not being able to speak "normally" to others and to the public. Keller did not support sign language as fervently as visual lipreading and speech. She was a longtime supporter of Alexander Graham Bell, a eugenicist and pioneer of oralism who believed that Deafness should be eradicated. Bell's life mission continues to harm Deaf people to this day.[5]

I mention Keller and part of her story here because social media platforms have recently mocked and questioned her lived experience.[6] Many non-disabled people continue to ask how a DeafBlind sensory experience or a life like Keller's is lived or if it is worth living at all. Thus, it is not d/Deafness or disability that cuts people off from the world; it is stigma and the design of the built environment through the lens of ableism. What if Keller had lived in a world that prioritized and celebrated how she felt and moved through it–a world designed to enhance her sensory pleasure?

The built environment is designed with only normative, non-disabled bodies in mind – bodies that hear sounds "perfectly," see all there is to see without difficulty, and move fluidly or unassisted through space as productive citizens. One must question whether the "normate" person even exists; yet, although there are an estimated 1.3 billion disabled people in the world, designers continue to create spaces that exclude disabled and Deaf people.[7] The fact that participation in social life relies so heavily on auditory information fundamentally differs from the reliance, emphasis, and manifestation of design through the visual, both in the process (e.g., drawing materials) and product. Both are ableist assumptions in that they depend on processing information in only one sensory mode: the verbal-auditory and the visual, respectively. What if designers stopped thinking about design and its everyday use in such definitive binaries? I rely almost entirely on visual design elements to wayfind, process information, and communicate. Still, I recognize the critical need to incorporate visual, auditory, and tactile (and even olfactory) sensory material into a site's design to create access and inclusion. This ideology applies not only to the built design but also to how it is produced. Instead of our typical two-dimensional drawings and renderings that we print on paper or display on a computer screen, what if we thought more about the tactile elements in illustrating our design intent? For example, Chris Downey, a Blind architect, creates his tactile architectural drawings and plans using innovative tools such as wax sticks and embossing printers.[8]

If Keller had lived in the late 20th century, as Downey and I have, perhaps she would not have been such a solitary and exceptional figure. She was able to thrive during her lifetime because of her racial and financial privileges. In the 1960s and 1970s, disabled people (without Keller's financial or familial resources) were finally being freed from institutions and asylums, banding together as a community and fighting for their collective rights. Keller would have been immersed in a world moving toward accessibility – if not yet in built form, then in policy and legislation. In 1973, Section 504 of the Federal Rehabilitation Act was passed and then ratified in 1977, requiring all federally funded buildings in the United States to be accessible to physically disabled people.[9] This was followed in 1990 by the Americans with Disabilities Act (ADA) and in 1991 by the ADA Standards for Accessible Design, which were most recently revised in 2010 (hereafter referred to as the *Standards*).

Unlike Keller, I am a member of the post-ADA generation: a fierce community of young disabled people born after the passage of the ADA who respect and honor the rights that our previous generations fought for–on behalf of all of us–while at the same time expecting and knowing that we deserve more. Without diminishing the importance of the ADA and the *Standards* in providing my broader disabled community and me with the right to access public spaces (which, I admit, I often take for granted), the ADA is approaching its 34th anniversary, and the *Standards* their 15th. Our fight for access continues, and it is high time to radically rethink accessibility in this country to include underrepresented members of the disabled community.[10]

People often ask what it is like to sense and experience a space "differently" as a Deaf person. Although it is difficult to describe without a point of comparison (my memory of pre-deafness, before I was eight years old, is vague), my experience of public spaces can be considered unique, whether navigating a sidewalk, exploring a park, or sitting in a plaza. My visual, tactile, and even olfactory senses are amplified. I am drawn to a place by its hues, its light, and its shadows; the textures and vibrations of the pavement beneath my feet; the coolness of water dappling in a fountain; the poignant scent of the earth and its blooms; or the aroma of freshly brewed coffee wafting through a plaza window. I rely on visual cues and cultural markers for navigation and the distinctive and tangible ways a space makes me feel. Thus, my experience of landscape does not require the ability to hear, but these experiences range from sublime pleasure–when my sensory experience is wonderfully aligned–to extreme irritation. When I wear my hearing aids in public spaces, I am overwhelmed by the noise overload, especially from traffic, large crowds, or boisterous music. If it is too bright, the glare hurts my eyes, and if it is too dark, the shadows strain them. Both prevent me from continuing a conversation comfortably (either by lipreading or using sign language). If the space is too exposed or cramped, I have to squeeze or contort my body or walk single-file on sidewalks, losing bits and pieces of the conversation. Smells can also overwhelm me much more than hearing people, whether it is the smell of rotting garbage in a trash can, dog urine on the sidewalk, or excessive gasoline fumes. Simply put, I gravitate to spaces where I feel particularly and effortlessly immersed in the essence of a place and where each individual space conforms to my body (and not the other way around) or can be easily adjusted to my comfort level through variety and choice.

Talking about sensory experience can be much more interesting than discussing legal and technical accessibility requirements. However, to illustrate the dual role of lived experience and accessibility requirements in sensing landscapes as a Deaf person–and the rather large discrepancies between the two–I will briefly discuss the nuances of specific legal requirements. The essential requirement of the ADA (as law) is to prohibit discrimination based on disability in employment, government, public accommodations, communications, transportation, and commercial facilities.[11] My work focuses primarily on going beyond the requirements of Title II of the ADA, State and Local Governments, which expands and clarifies the original requirements of Section 504 of the Federal Rehabilitation Act of 1973 and includes public spaces (i.e., cities and planning, streetscapes, and publicly owned landscapes such as parks and plazas).[12]

Although the *Standards* have been a tremendous achievement in creating a more accessible United States, they focus predominantly on the needs of wheelchair users and people who are Blind or have low vision, leaving little room for deviation from the standard measurements adopted for use. In other words, even disability has been standardized to some extent.[13] There is little mention of the Deaf and hard-of-hearing community and no mention of autistic or neurodivergent people, people with neurocognitive disabilities, or people with other types of physical or mobility disabilities, psychological disabilities, or chronic illnesses (nor any combination of the above disabilities, as many people have more than one).

Disability rights expert Dr. Victor Santiago Pineda makes this narrow scope clear:

> Although the legal definition of disability used in the ADA calls attention to a diverse set of mental and physical conditions that can be considered debilitating relative to the general population–and it is among the most progressive in the world–it falls short of informing a radical understanding of disability that accounts for the relationship between an individual and their environment.[14]

Thus, not only does the ADA fail to fully account for the broad range of experiences of disabled people, but it also fails to challenge "normative" and discriminatory assumptions about the built environment, including about disability itself. Designer and researcher Dr. Aimi Hamraie further clarifies, "The ADA has not resulted in a postdiscrimination world...normal, taken-for-granted aspects of built environments, such as the prevalence of stairs, work in tandem with discriminatory attitudes."[15] With such a wide range of experiences of disabled people juxtaposed with narrow ableist assumptions, our legal requirements and guidance for creating accessible and inclusive design are limited. For this reason, existing legal requirements should only be considered as a baseline or a foundation to build upon in the design process.[16]

As a baseline, the *Standards* are intended to protect the general public's safety and ensure effective access to both the built environment and communication.[17] For the Deaf and hard-of-hearing communities, full access to communication means accommodating visual communication such as ASL (which may include tactile ASL for DeafBlind people), lipreading, captioning, and/or supplementing auditory information with amplification for those who rely on residual hearing. One would assume that Deaf and hard-of-hearing people would thrive in any environment with this legal requirement of "effective access to communication." Although Deaf people do passively benefit from many of the design requirements of the *Standards* (e.g., sidewalk width and slope requirements, limitation of obstructions, color contrast, signage requirements), this specific federal legal requirement regarding access

1 Douglas C. Baynton, "Deafness," in Rachel Adams, Benjamin Reiss & David Serlin (eds), *Keywords for Disability Studies* (New York University Press, 2015), 147–55.

2 For more on the medical vs. social models of disability, refer to Victor Santiago Pineda, "Enabling Justice: Spatializing Disability in the Built Environment," *Critical Planning Journal* 15, Summer (2008): 110–23, and Alexa Vaughn, Design with Disabled People Now, "How to Talk to and About Disabled People in the Design Process," https://www.designwithdisabledpeoplenow.com/language (accessed November 7, 2023).

3 John V. Van Cleve, ed., *Gallaudet Encyclopedia of Deaf People and Deafness*, Vol. 2 (McGraw-Hill, 1987), 125.

4 Arlene Balkansky, "Helen Keller: Activist and Orator," *Library of Congress Blogs* (July 31, 2018), https://blogs.loc.gov/headlinesandheroes/2018/07/helen-keller/.

5 For more eugenicist history on Bell, refer to Katie Booth, *The Invention of Miracles: Language, Power, and Alexander Graham Bell's Quest to End Deafness* (Simon and Schuster, 2021).

6 Seren Morris, "TikTok Awash with Bizarre Videos Questioning Whether Helen Keller Existed," *Newsweek* (January 6, 2021), https://www.newsweek.com/tiktok-bizarre-videos-questioning-whether-helen-keller-existed-1559296.

7 For more on the concept of the "normate" and the "normate template" and the "ideal" or "universal" body, refer to Aimi Hamraie, "Chapter 1: Normate Template: Knowing-Making the Architectural Inhabitant," in *Building Access: Universal Design and the Politics of Disability* (University of Minnesota Press, 2017), 19–39.

8 Erin Donnelly, "How Blind Architect Chris Downey Keeps Working," *Azure* (December 15, 2016), https://www.azuremagazine.com/article/blind-architect-chris-downey/.

9 For more on the history of disability and the protest for the passage of Section 504, refer to Kitty Cone, Disability Rights Education and Defense Fund, "Short History of the 504 Sit-in," https://dredf.org/504-sit-in-20th-anniversary/short-history-of-the-504-sit-in/ (accessed November 8, 2023).

10 Alexa Vaughn, "The ADA at 30: The Battle for an Accessible and Inclusive Future Continues," *The Dirt* (July 24, 2020), https://dirt.asla.org/2020/07/24/.

11 US Department of Justice Civil Rights Division, "Guide to Disability Rights Laws," https://www.ada.gov/resources/disability-rights-guide/ (accessed December 20, 2023).

12 There is an opportunity to apply the same philosophy to Title III: Places of Public Accommodation, which includes privately owned spaces with some public use. In addition, the *Architectural Barriers Act (ABA) Standards*, the *California Building Code (CBC-11B)*, and the *Public Rights-of-Way Accessibility Guidelines* are relevant to my work.

13 Refer again to Hamraie on the "Normate Template" in *Building Access*, 19–39.

14 Pineda, "Enabling Justice," 112–13.

15 Hamraie, *Building Access*, 3.

Flashing Fire Alarms

According to Section 702 of the *Standards*, emergency warning and alarm systems in buildings must have permanent audible and visible components that comply with NFPA 72 (the *National Fire Alarm and Signaling Code*), although the sound level must not exceed 110 dB (still inaudible to some Deaf people but can cause hearing damage to hearing people).[1] The visible element is a flashing strobe light on the alarm that makes the alarm signal visible when the smoke from a fire triggers it. Flashing fire alarms are integral to the safety and welfare of Deaf and hard-of-hearing people, but they are not typically required for exterior spaces and do not affect the built form.

1 Department of Justice, "Chapter 7: Communication Elements and Features" and "Chapter 8: Special Rooms, Spaces, and Elements," *The ADA Standards for Accessible Design* (September 15, 2010), 186, 211.

2 Ibid., "Chapter 2: Scoping Requirements," 76–77; "Chapter 7: Communication Elements and Features," 194–98.

3 Refer to US Department of Justice Civil Rights Division, "Guide to Disability Rights Laws," https://www.ada.gov/resources/disability-rights-guide/#telecommunications-act (accessed December 20, 2023).

4 Department of Justice, "Chapter 1: Application and Administration" and "Chapter 7: Communication Elements and Features," *The ADA Standards for Accessible Design* (September 15, 2010), 48, 196.

Assistive Listening Systems

Assistive listening systems (and their related devices) are required in assembly areas and must comply with Section 706.[2] The *Standards* classify assembly areas as stadiums, arenas, grandstands, amphitheaters, and indoor theaters or performance venues. Assistive listening systems have several types of transmission, including wired and wireless (e.g., induction loop, infrared, and FM radio). As per Section 219, assistive listening systems must be provided when "audible communication is integral to the use of the space" and when audio amplification is used in the venue. The amount required varies, and some must be compatible with hearing aids.

In general, assistive listening systems and devices benefit many hard-of-hearing people who rely on residual hearing. Personally, these devices do not help me understand spoken language. I would rather wear my personal hearing aids than an assistive listening device, and I still need live captioning or interpretation to be fully accommodated. Many Deaf people have no residual hearing and therefore do not rely on it for communication. Furthermore, these systems have little to no use or value in public spaces; they cannot be installed on public sidewalks or in parks or plazas away from large venues.

Teletypewriters (TTYs)

The Deaf and hard-of-hearing communities and people with speech disabilities have particularly benefited from Title IV: Telecommunications Access. This title extended civil rights protections through video and text relay services for TTYs and closed captioning for federally funded public service announcements.[3] A TTY device enables interactive text-based communication through coded signals over a telephone network and must be made available alongside public pay telephones with various installation requirements.[4] TTYs were developed in the 1960s by Robert Weitbrecht, a Deaf American scientist. They were novel at the time, allowing Deaf and hard-of-hearing people to make independent phone calls to each other and to hearing people for the first time in history. Relay service was limited until the late 1980s, when it was mandated by various states, and then expanded in 1990 to be federally mandated by the ADA. Today, anyone can use a TTY relay by dialing 711.

Although TTY phones are still used by many Deaf and hard-of-hearing people, they have become archaic, as they have been phased out by video relay phones and smartphones with Facetime or video messaging, texting, and visual voicemail capabilities, as well as advances in live captioning—for landlines, smartphones, and other platforms like Zoom—with options for live person captioning and AI. I have never seen a TTY installed at a public payphone, nor are there many public payphones that are still intact. I have tried dialing 711 on my smartphone several times, but the call has failed. Thus, the TTY becomes a somewhat limited (and possibly unusable and unenforced) standard that does not affect the design of outdoor public spaces.

to communication falls short: How, if at all, is effective access to communication manifested and guaranteed by built form in the public realm?

Effective access to visual communication–ensuring that Deaf and hard-of-hearing people can comfortably move through and use space while relying on visual communication such as ASL–has not yet been required, enforced, or consciously achieved through design in the broader public landscape. Legal standards for creating effective access to communication have only been applied to interiors, products, and technologies in limited ways, namely through three specific requirements outlined in the *Standards*: flashing fire alarms, assistive listening systems, and teletypewriters (TTYs). In other words, the creation of access for Deaf and hard-of-hearing people has focused on technological and interior design implementations, not on the design of exterior public spaces. Although this would imply that accessibility has moved further to the forefront of the work of architects (rather than landscape architects), this is not the case: legally required interior applications often remain limited and outdated, as secondary, non-innovative "band-aids" to ensure that the bare minimum of safety and technological requirements are met, rather than incorporating spatial preferences. Meanwhile, new guidelines and standards for exterior spaces (e.g., the Public Rights-of-Way Guidelines) still require more direct feedback from stakeholders with sensory and neurocognitive disabilities.

Public Rights-of-Way Accessibility Guidelines

The history of the *Public Rights-of-Way Accessibility Guidelines (PROWAG)* spans more than 20 years, beginning in 1999 with the establishment of the PROWAG Advisory Committee by the US Access Board. Although the proposed draft guidelines were released for public comment in 2013, the final rule was not published until recently, in August 2023, illustrating the excruciatingly long process of creating change in federal access law. *PROWAG* addresses the statutory requirements of the ADA (as law) and the Architectural Barriers Act (ABA) and fills significant regulatory gaps. This includes more extensive provisions and detailed guidance for large stretches of streetscape and sidewalks, including on-street parking, pedestrian signals, crosswalks, and curb ramps, which are not as thoroughly addressed in the *Standards* and which some states have already gone somewhat beyond.[18]

For example, pedestrian access routes must be at least 48 inches wide (excluding curb width) and 60 inches wide where pedestrian access routes cross medians (or at least as wide as the crosswalk, which is 60 inches or wider). If the route is reduced to less than 60 inches, passing areas at least 60 inches wide must be provided every 200 feet.[19] These guidelines go beyond those listed in the *Standards*, which require a clear width of only 36 inches.[20] However, *PROWAG* has not yet been adopted by the Department of Justice or the Department of Transportation, so it is not legally enforceable. Although *PROWAG* provides additional space for movement on sidewalks, it is still inadequate for Deaf and hard-of-hearing people who rely on visual communication and would benefit from sidewalks that are at least six- to ten-feet wide.

My original work in designing for the Deaf and hard-of-hearing community–"DeafScape: Applying DeafSpace to Landscape"–appeared in *Ground Up Journal* in 2018.[21] At the time, I was a graduate student at the University of California, Berkeley, and had just arrived at my dual identity as a Deaf woman and a landscape designer. Since then, the piece has been featured in numerous publications. I have expanded the concept by creating new graphics, compilations of built case studies, lectures, accessibility audits, and exhibitions, as well as independent consulting, practice, and fellowships. The work continues to be informed by lived experience – my own and that of other Deaf, hard-of-hearing, and disabled people. Gallaudet University's 2010 *DeafSpace Design Guidelines (DSDG)* remain the primary inspiration and

16 Alexa Vaughn, Design with Disabled People Now, "How to Design Beyond the ADA," https://www.designwithdisabledpeoplenow.com/design-beyond-ada (accessed December 20, 2023).

17 US Department of Justice Civil Rights Division, "ADA Requirements: Effective Communication," https://www.ada.gov/resources/effective-communication/ (accessed December 20, 2023).

18 As a Californian, I am familiar with the requirements for outdoor public spaces (*California Building Code*, or *CBC-11B*), which in many cases go beyond the requirements of the *ADA Standards*. For example, Section 705 requires detectable warning surfaces (also known as truncated domes, which are usually yellow) to be installed at all curb ramps at crosswalks, whereas the *ADA Standards* only require their installation at public transportation facilities and platforms. The new *PROWAG* provides guidance for their placement at all curb ramps but is not yet legally required.

19 US Access Board, "Chapter 3: Technical Requirements," *Public Right-of-Way Accessibility Guidelines* (August 8, 2023), https://www.access-board.gov/prowag/technical.html.

20 Department of Justice, "Chapter 4: Accessible Routes," *The ADA Standards for Accessible Design* (September 15, 2010), 117.

21 Alexa Vaughn, "DeafScape: Applying DeafSpace to Landscape," *Ground Up Journal* 7 (2018): 100–3.

22 Hansel Bauman, *DeafSpace Design Guidelines*, Vol. 1 (Working Draft, 2010).

23 Ellen Lupton, "Sensory Environments," in Ellen Lupton & Andrea Lipps (eds), *The Senses: Design Beyond Vision* (Princeton Architectural Press with Cooper Hewitt, 2018), 124.

24 Sara Weissman, "Building Up the Black Deaf Student Community," *Inside Higher Ed* (December 20, 2023), https://www.insidehighered.com/news/students/diversity/2023/12/20/gallaudet-adds-resources-specifically-black-deaf-students. Refer also to Gallaudet University, "The Louise B. Miller Memorial," https://gallaudet.edu/the-memorial/ (accessed January 5, 2024).

"If I don't rest
in public
my world gets
very very small."
Raquel

method for creating landscapes and urban spaces that are not only accessible to Deaf and hard-of-hearing people, but that transcend the ADA and center our comfort, preferences, and joy.[22] The principles are radical in that they involved the Deaf and hard-of-hearing community at Gallaudet in the creation process. In DeafSpace, "sensory details highlight human presence" to affirm and celebrate Deafness.[23] Unfortunately, the *DSDG* was never formally published or distributed. However, through my ongoing work, I have aimed to share its principles and ethos in applications to landscape architecture and urban design.

Considering the previous discussion of the *Standards* and *PROWAG*, it is clear that the creation of access for Deaf and hard-of-hearing people has focused on technological and interior implementations, not on the design of exterior spaces in the public realm. In order to center the Deaf sensory experience (360° around the body) and visual language such as sign language and lipreading, designers need to go beyond the legal requirements by continuing to incorporate direct feedback from the Deaf community alongside the application of DeafSpace/DeafScape principles. This would allow for better visual communication and more space for movement by creating areas free of obstructions and tripping hazards (e.g., wider paths and ramps or sloped walkways) and additional space adjacent to primary paths to pause or communicate (e.g., eddies and shoulder zones).

Wayfinding would also be prioritized to create a visual and tactile language for understanding the space and facilitating safe movement (e.g., landmarks, rhythm, tactile cues, and visual cues). A variety of furnishings would increase the sense of comfort and safety and enhance visual communication (e.g., flexible and fixed furnishings, degrees of enclosure, and U-shaped or circular seating). Glare would be reduced during the day, while visibility would be increased at night to reduce eye strain (e.g., through shade and night lighting). Many of these principles are already unintentionally applied to landscape architecture designs in public and private areas, but often in a piecemeal fashion. It is rare for many or all of these principles to be applied holistically in a space, and even rarer for Deaf and hard-of-hearing designers and stakeholders to be directly involved in the design process.

Sensing landscapes is different for everyone, whether Deaf or hearing, disabled or non-disabled, and sensory experience is often not easily defined by typical or normative spatial parameters, scales, or descriptions. As DeafScape demonstrates, landscape architects and urban designers can radically change how we design our cities and enrich the way each of us can experience and enjoy public spaces by celebrating our differences and honoring our commitment to the lived experiences of Deaf and disabled stakeholders over assumptions about them. Not only must we continue to reckon with ableist assumptions in design, but also racist and sexist assumptions. For example, Gallaudet University has begun to rethink the limitations of the original *DeafSpace Design Guidelines* by designing, with and for the Black Deaf community, a memorial to Louise B. Miller (a Black mother who fought for the rights to education of Black Deaf children, including her own, during segregation), by supporting the teaching and use of Black American Sign Language (BASL), and by expanding its Center for Black Deaf Studies.[24] There is still much work to be done in designing for intersectionality, but when applied holistically and intentionally, the principles of DeafSpace/DeafScape celebrate and enhance the Deaf experience in the landscape rather than stifle it. Our work does not end with the *Standards*; it is just beginning. Only when a variety of lived experiences are validated and prioritized can we grow in our understanding and claim responsibility for designing spaces where Deaf and disabled people can fully experience sensory joy.

Opposite: *Resting Conversations* by Raquel Meseguer Zafe and Helen Stratford, Postman's Park, London (2023).

AUDIBLE CARTOGRAPHIES OF POWER
GASCIA OUZOUNIAN

Gascia Ouzounian is a sonic theorist and practitioner whose work explores sound in relation to histories of science and technology, space, urbanism, and violence. She is the author of *Stereophonica: Sound and Space in Science, Technology, and the Arts* (MIT Press). Ouzounian is an associate professor of music at the University of Oxford, where she directs the European Research Council-funded project "Sonorous Cities: Toward a Sonic Urbanism" (soncities.org).

+ MUSIC, CARTOGRAPHY

On the surface, sound might seem antithetical to mapping, its dynamic flows and temporality resistant to the fixity of the map. A sound map that describes something as vast and always-fluctuating as a city raises even more questions: if sound is evanescent, changing from moment to moment in uncontrollable and unpredictable ways before permanently fading, and if it is radically localized, "tied" to a source and therefore always contingent upon the movements or actions of that source, then how can it be mapped at all?

The tensions inherent in merging the flows of sound–a medium whose material nature is most commonly represented as a wave–with the durability of the map emerge in intriguing ways, particularly in sound maps that contend with a third, unpredictable element: power, and how power relations shape the sonic environments of cities.

Sound maps have existed in various forms for centuries across geographical and cultural contexts. In "Ephemeral Cartography" (2018), the musicologist Peter McMurray finds sound maps in such varied cultural traditions as Kaluli women's creation of verbal maps to mourn the deceased and the *mappae mundi* of early modern Europe, whose imagery and texts evoke sounds and allude to hearing.[1] McMurray's helpful taxonomy of sound maps includes mapping *in* sound, as in artworks and compositions that sonically "map" a site; mapping *by* sound, as with the mapping of underwater environments using sonar; and the mapping *of* sound, as in maps that depict sonic environments or "soundscapes."

It is the last of these that I seek to explore here: first, because of the tensions inherent in mapping sound; second, because of the recent proliferation of such maps despite these tensions; and third, because maps of soundscapes can reveal aspects of environments, including cities, that would otherwise go unnoticed and unremarked. Listening to the city through sound maps–under-examined tools for what Shannon Mattern has called "urban auscultation"–can transform broader understandings of both sound and mapping, revealing urban soundscapes not as neutral sites comprised of various sounds that can be heard, recorded, and scientifically analyzed (a predominating paradigm in soundscape studies) but as contested territories in which power relations can become evident through mapping.[2]

Noise Mapping in Perspective

While various modes of mapping *in* sound have existed for centuries, the mapping *of* sound environments, and in particular of urban soundscapes, first emerged in a concerted way in the 1930s, a period marked by rapid urbanization, industrialization, and, concomitantly, rising levels of environmental noise. Early noise maps (maps of loudness levels or "noise levels") of cities were typically hand-drawn street maps or topographical maps that showed the average noise levels of individual city streets or urban districts as measured in decibels or phons.

As sound historian James Mansell has shown, this period was equally marked by a growing hysteria around noise, including the idea that noise could cause neurasthenia or nervous collapse.[3] This was particularly relevant for dense cities whose soundscapes were marked by high levels of industrial, construction, and transportation noise; indeed, neurasthenia was also sometimes called "Londonitis." A rumor held that cities would eventually deafen their inhabitants if noise levels continued to rise by one decibel per year, a much-repeated but erroneous figure. Municipal authorities thus began to commission the production of noise maps to track rising noise levels and to address this growing public health concern.[4] Their efforts redoubled in the 1950s and 1960s in connection with the rapid growth of commercial flights, which presented a new noise threat from the sky. It was during this period that noise began to be understood not merely as a *nuisance*–what might be addressed by eliminating particular sources of noise such as tugboat whistles (the subject of the first anti-noise ordinance in the United States)—but, increasingly, as a *pollutant*: as something "in the air," pervasive, inescapable, and, importantly, capable of breaching the barriers of the human body. As a pollutant, one inextricable from the very atmosphere of the city, noise required "global" solutions: lowering overall noise levels through zoning laws, for example, instead of targeting individual noise sources.

Today, the noise mapping of cities has become routine and, in many places, is enforced by law. In the European Union, for example, the Environmental Noise Directive of 2002 stipulated that by 2012, every municipality with a population size of over 100,000 must produce strategic noise maps to assess noise exposure and overall noise levels.[5] Such noise maps are accompanied by action plans that describe how city authorities will mitigate the exposure of urban populations to harmful levels of noise, which has been linked to a variety of negative outcomes, from poor performance in school to miscarriage, hearing loss, and heart disease.

Noise mapping is increasingly technologically sophisticated, and noise maps have become much more varied in what they can depict. In contrast to the hand-drawn maps of the 1930s, whose data were gathered by taking individual noise level readings using handheld acoustimeters or audiometers, the noise maps commissioned by municipal authorities today are software-generated *models* of noise environments that draw on large datasets pertaining to road, air, and railway noise, which, along with construction and industrial noise, constitute the main sources of urban noise.

Software-generated noise maps might be three-dimensional—showing noise levels both in the horizontal and vertical domains—such as by depicting noise level variation not only at street level but also rising through the floors of a skyscraper, and they might be dynamic and interactive, with users able to control for such parameters as the presence of noise barriers. Furthermore, some specialist noise maps produced in the context of scientific research projects are not based on noise *modeling* but are rather generated in real time using audio data collected by sensors: microphones installed on city streets, as in the Sounds of New York City (SONYC) project, or microphones embedded in cellphones, as in NoiseSPY.[6]

Artificial intelligence, citizen science, and machine listening have contributed to a noise mapping landscape in which noise maps can depict not only noise levels but also actual noises that are present in the city. Machine listening algorithms can confidently distinguish between a "car honking," "construction noise," a "dog barking," and a "gunshot." A noise map derived from cellphone data might even trace urban residents' movements through a city, showing how different individuals' exposure to noise varies as they navigate various urban districts.

Such developments in noise mapping are notable not only because they might inform policymaking or help local authorities to respond more efficiently to noise complaints but also because they show how exposure to noise changes at the level of the individual and across various urban districts. These latter features are an important step toward understanding noise in connection with socioeconomic inequalities: how urban residents are differently exposed to harmful levels of noise based on differences in income, ethnicity, place of work, and place of residence, for example. As such, the ever-more-granular and individuated mapping of noise can help us to understand unequal noise exposure better and thus to confront what Nathalie Harb, whose installation *The Silent Room* (2017) addresses how noise affects different groups to different degrees, has powerfully identified as a form of social injustice.[7]

Urban Sound Maps

Alongside technological advances in noise mapping, artists and researchers have become increasingly attuned to the need for maps that depict not only urban noise

1 Peter McMurray, "Ephemeral Cartography: On Mapping Sound," *Sound Studies* 4, no. 2 (2018): 110–42.

2 Shannon Mattern, "Urban Auscultation; or, Perceiving the Action of the Heart," *Places Journal* (April 2020), https://placesjournal.org/article/urban-auscultation-or-perceiving-the-action-of-the-heart.

3 James G. Mansell, *The Age of Noise in Britain: Hearing Modernity* (University of Illinois Press, 2016).

4 Gascia Ouzounian, *Stereophonica: Sound and Space in Science, Technology, and the Arts* (MIT Press, 2021).

5 European Commission, Directive 2002/49/EC of the European Parliament and of the Council. Assessment and Management of Environmental Noise. *Official Journal of the European Communities*, L 189/12-L 189/25.

6 Sounds of New York City (SONYC), https://wp.nyu.edu/sonyc/ (accessed October 23, 2023); Eiman Kanjo, "NoiseSPY: A Real-Time Mobile Phone Platform for Urban Noise Monitoring and Mapping," *Mobile Networks and Applications* 15, no. 4 (2010): 562–74.

7 Nathalie Harb, *Silent Room* V0.1, https://nathalieharb.com/portfolio/silentroomvo1/ (accessed October 23, 2023).

8 Raymond Murray Schafer, *The Book of Noise* (Price Milburn & Co., 1970).

9 Peter Cusack, *Favourite Sounds* (1998–ongoing), https://crisap.org/research/projects/favourite-sounds/ (accessed October 23, 2023).

10 Max Stein & Julian Stein, *Montréal Sound Map* (2008–ongoing), https://www.montrealsoundmap.com/ (accessed October 23, 2023).

11 Allie Martin, *Go-Go Mapping in Washington, DC* (2015–ongoing), http://blacksoundlab.com/mapping/ (accessed October 23, 2023).

12 Allie Martin, Black Sound Lab–About, https://blacksoundlab.com/about/ (accessed October 23, 2023).

13 Alexander Holmes, Social Housing Sound Archive, https://www.socialhousingsoundarchive.com/ (accessed October 23, 2023).

14 Alexander Holmes, Social Housing Sound Archive–About, https://www.socialhousingsoundarchive.com/about (accessed October 23, 2023).

15 Anna Raimondo, To Listen, http://annaraimondo.com/listen/ (accessed October 23, 2023).

16 Anna Feigenbaum & Anja Kanngieser, "For a Politics of Atmospheric Governance," *Dialogues in Human Geography* 5, no. 1 (2015): 81.

17 Gernot Böhme, *Atmospheric Architectures: The Aesthetics of Felt Spaces*, trans. Anna-Christina Engels-Schwarzpaul (Bloomsbury Academic, 2017).

18 Feigenbaum & Kanngieser, "For a Politics of Atmospheric Governance," 83.

19 Lawrence Abu Hamdan & Earshot, *Air Pressure*, https://www.airpressure.info/ (accessed October 23, 2023).

but also the rich, varied, and changing soundscapes of cities. Animating their efforts are such questions as how can sound maps (maps depicting soundscapes as opposed to noise levels) illuminate such urban processes as gentrification and displacement? Are specific urban communities or groups privileged or disadvantaged in shaping urban soundscapes and thus participating in the acoustic life of a city? What can mapping bring to our understanding of the social and political dimensions of urban sound?

Early sound maps of cities, including the corpus of sound maps created by the World Soundscape Project (WSP), an influential research group founded in the late 1960s by the Canadian composer R. Murray Schafer, were underpinned by concerns around acoustic ecology: the study and conservation of sonic environments to increase their "health." This could mean, for example, tracking the sonic markers of biodiversity, such as the presence of birdsong or other animal sounds, or undertaking longitudinal studies of soundscapes to determine how they have changed over time. The WSP's efforts in sound mapping and noise mapping were also tied to concerns about noise pollution. Indeed, in his earliest writings, including *The Book of Noise* (1970), Schafer was adamant that cities, sites marked by "technological" and "man-made" noise, threatened the well-being of listeners.[8]

Nevertheless, sound mapping projects that emerged from acoustic ecology have also drawn attention to the positive aspects of urban soundscapes. The artist Peter Cusack's online sound map *Favourite Sounds* (1998–ongoing), for example, invites participants to respond to the question "What is your favourite sound of [city] and why?" The replies, writes Cusack, "[reveal] both the city of the ear and the significant role that everyday sounds play in our lives."[9] Max Stein and Julian Stein, the creators of the online, interactive *Montréal Sound Map* (2008–ongoing), specifically promote an "optimistic approach to acoustic ecology."[10] Such efforts, which invite the wider public to contribute sound recordings of urban soundscapes, are essential for raising consciousness about an often-overlooked dimension of urban environments. Equally, they help to counter discourses that equate urban sound solely with noise: unwanted sound that should be reduced, controlled, or mitigated.

More recently, artists and researchers have developed urban sound mapping projects that function as counter-maps, offering counter-narratives to official or hegemonic narratives of urban spaces, communities, and histories. With *Mapping Go-Go Music in Washington, DC* (2015–ongoing), ethnomusicologist Allie Martin, director of the Black Sound Lab research hub at Dartmouth College, maps the effects of gentrification through its audible traces.[11] This series of online maps depicts the displacement of Go-Go venues in Washington, DC over a period of 50 years between 1970 and 2020. One map shows how a wealthier and whiter DC corresponds to the displacement of Go-Go–what Martin describes as a genre of funk music native to Black communities in DC–from the city center to its outskirts and away from historically Black neighborhoods as well as vital urban cultural infrastructures.

Whereas most online sound maps "pin" environmental sound recordings to an interactive, online map powered by an open-source mapping API such as Google Maps, a map like Martin's does not use sound recordings to engage urban soundscapes. Instead, it draws on census data–in this case, data about income and race–to show how gentrification correlates with changing urban soundscapes in ways that are demonstrably racialized and classed.

Notably, Martin's mapping project coincided with the #DontMuteDC movement, a local activist movement that aimed to recover Go-Go music as a vital part of DC's intangible cultural heritage during a period of rapid gentrification and ousters of Black communities. As Martin writes, part of her larger mission with Black Sound Lab is not only to document such changes using digital mapping techniques but also to actively "decriminalize Black sound": to "work against policies that proceed to harm Black people over sonic expression that has been deemed too noisy, loud, and dangerous."[12]

Tracing gentrification through changing urban soundscapes similarly animates the Social Housing Sonic Archive, an archive of disappearing sounds of social housing in London by the musician and recordist A. J. Holmes.[13] For Holmes, a lifelong resident of social housing in London, the archive is a means to preserve the sonic cultures, voices, accents, and environments of working-class communities that have been displaced through housing policies that disadvantage low-income residents. Holmes's project also has an activist aim: by collecting the disappearing sounds of social housing estates, he advocates for an end to what he calls the "inhumane social cleansing that is currently taking place under the guise of so-called 'regeneration' schemes."[14]

Urban sound maps that focus on sociopolitical issues might equally reveal aspects of the city that otherwise escape the gaze of urban studies. Since 2017, the artist-researcher Anna Raimondo's series of feminist urban sound maps have invited female-identifying residents of cities that include Rome, Valparaíso, Santa Cruz de Tenerife, and Lucena to share their experiences of those cities in relation to gender, sexuality, class, race, and citizenship.[15] The project, which combines illustrated maps of participants' statements with performances, sound installations, and sound recordings, reveals gendered perspectives of the city mapped through women's voices. There are troubling commonalities across the maps: shared experiences of marginalization, sexual harassment, and exclusion from "public" spaces that are, in practice, still treated as the exclusive domain of men.

Cartographies of Pressure

In "For a Politics of Atmospheric Governance" (2015), Anna Feigenbaum and A. M. Kanngieser propose the idea of

"atmospheric policing" to describe "those technologies and techniques for controlling populations that are fundamentally predicated on their relationship with air."[16] The policing of classed and racialized sounds in gentrifying cities–such as forbidding the playback of Go-Go music in a public space where it had previously played for decades in response to a noise complaint by a wealthy new resident, an event that triggered the #DontMuteDC movement–can be considered a form of atmospheric policing. Sound is inextricable from air and atmosphere: sounds propagate through the air, and, borrowing from Gernot Böhme, sound profoundly shapes the "aesthetics of atmosphere."[17] An analysis of how sonic environments are designed and produced could thus meaningfully form part of an emergent critique of urban atmospherics.

Feigenbaum and Kanngieser specifically call for a more robust critique of "how atmospheres function as part of broader political systems of discipline and containment."[18] They discuss sonic warfare–which might include the use of sound weapons such as stun grenades and sonic booms, or the use of threatening or alarming sounds–as a form of atmospheric policing. While explosive and spectacularly violent forms of sonic warfare have come under increasing scrutiny in recent years as methods of punishment and control, ambient sounds that do not cause harm through loudness, but which nevertheless permeate the air and alter the atmosphere, can also signal uneven power relations and even constitute a form of atmospheric violence.

Such a form of atmospheric violence comes to the fore in Lawrence Abu Hamdan's *Air Pressure*, a wide-ranging project with the audio investigative agency Earshot that tracks the illegal presence of Israeli military aircraft over Lebanese airspace since 2007.[19] So far, the project has identified 22,355 airspace violations by Israeli aircraft between 2007 and 2023 [it is updated every year]. A website, airpressure.info, features an interactive map that plots the trajectories of every Israeli aircraft identified in UN documents as violating Lebanese airspace, and a page that collects the sounds of those aircraft, which are principally "spotted" by civilians through the sounds they make. As Abu Hamdan said in a recent lecture on the project, "in most videos [by civilians] you don't see a dot [[aircraft]]. You only hear the sky rumbling."[20] He writes:

> Constantly hearing hostile jets and drones overhead, residents of Lebanon live in a state of precarity; the potential of full-scale aerial bombardment is a daily possibility. The disturbing roar of Fighter jets tearing up the coastline and the persistent buzz of Unmanned Aerial Vehicles circling the southern regions have become a familiar part of the Lebanese soundscape.[21]

For Abu Hamdan, that these sounds have become familiar constitutes a particular kind of harm: "its mundanity is part of what makes it so violent. People ignoring it is part of what makes it so violent," he says.[22] The type of violence these sounds represent is one that Abu Hamdan describes as "the theft of the future. That noise signals: *don't plan, don't think. It [an aerial invasion] can happen anytime*."[23] He describes the map of airspace violations as a "cartography of pressure."[24] Methods of containment and control are signaled and exerted through changes in air pressure and sound pressure, and everyday life is altered through what Abu Hamdan calls the "militarization of ambient sound."[25] This recalls Feigenbaum and Kanngieser's claim that "atmospheres of terror are built through the escalation of military governance into the air in which everyday life is enveloped."[26]

Mapping Acoustic Territories

The mapping of urban sound environments first emerged as a tool for assessing noise levels in industrializing cities and later developed as a way of documenting changing soundscapes. Today, sound maps exceed their original bureaucratic, scientific, historical, archival, or ecological purposes. Through maps such as *Mapping Go-Go Music in Washington, DC* and *Air Pressure*, soundscapes emerge as contested territories in which power relations are expressed: as sites of diverse, intersecting, and competing sonic cultures that may be differentially policed or managed and as sites in and through which governments and authorities assert power and exert control.

Through such projects, which contend with such immaterial elements as sound and air, mapping also extends beyond delimiting territories; it becomes a way of setting into relation phenomena that might not otherwise be understood as related, as in the disappearance of a Black musical tradition from a gentrifying city; or a way of revealing hidden patterns, including patterns of violence and inequality, as in maps of airspace violations or uneven noise exposure in cities. More broadly, these maps are a way of making audible something as slippery as power as it shapes something as intangible as sound. As audible cartographies of power, they reveal the acoustic city as an unstable, always-evolving territory deeply intertwined with the fluxes and flows of power.

20 Lawrence Abu Hamdan, "400 Billion Dollars of Air," Lecture at the Royal College of Art, London, October 11, 2023.

21 Abu Hamdan & Earshot, *Air Pressure*.

22 Abu Hamdan, "400 Billion Dollars of Air."

23 Ibid.

24 Ibid.

25 Ibid.

26 Feigenbaum & Kanngieser, "For a Politics of Atmospheric Governance," 83.

Acknowledgments
This article was funded by the European Research Council (ERC), under the European Union's Horizon 2020 research and innovation program, as part of the project "Sonorous Cities: Towards a Sonic Urbanism" (Grant Agreement No. 865032).

GRILL
LARSON CO.
The Original
STREET STOR
MATTRESS
BOX SPRING
$35.50
12th Street Store
MAXWELL ST
1330 S
{BRACKET ROOM}
{BRACKET ROOM}
SPORTS LOUNGE & EATERY

TIM CRESSWELL

SENSES OF PLACE

Tim Cresswell is Ogilvie Professor of Geography at the University of Edinburgh. He is a cultural geographer by training and the author or editor of a dozen books and over 100 articles on the role of space, place, and mobility in social and cultural life. Cresswell is also a widely published poet with three collections – most recently *Plastiglomerate* (Penned in the Margins, 2020).

+ GEOGRAPHY, URBAN DESIGN

Place is a slippery concept. It is at once obvious, something we can all relate to, and complicated, thanks to its multitude of uses by geographers, architects, philosophers, and planners. Recently it has become ubiquitous in the phrase "place-making," which has been used by planners, corporations, architects, and others to denote an interest in something more than making buildings or material spaces. But what is this "more than"? Partly the answer is an investment in people and community, in both decision-making processes and the actual design of spaces. Most obviously, place-making signals an interest in worlds of meaning and liveliness that come with taking people seriously. These are two aspects of what has long been called sense of place. The idea of place encompasses location (the where of something), locale (the physical presence or landscape of a place), and sense of place (the subjective and meaningful component of place). Of these, the last is probably the hardest to grapple with when accounting for existing places or engaging in processes of place-making.

Consider meaning and liveliness in turn. The geographer Yi-Fu Tuan referred to places as "centers of meaning" and "fields of care."[1] Meaning and care can arise from both individual and shared, or mediated, experience. Our biographies are often profoundly place-bound. The places we grew up in, fell in love in, went to school in, or even worked in, can resonate throughout our lives and we might feel a strong sense of place when we revisit them or think about them. They may mean nothing to others around us, but a lot to us. But places themselves are also said to have senses of place that are in some way shared, and it is this kind of sense that place-makers are attempting to engineer. A location that is said to exhibit a sense of place is one that is assumed to resonate with many people. There appears to be agreement that some kinds of places definitely have a sense of place. These are usually places with deep histories or lively presences – marketplaces, old town squares, monumental places. Some senses of place are mediated so widely that we all feel it. Few, for instance, would claim that Paris lacks a sense of place, even if the city of light and romance often becomes the kinds of montaged cliché we see in TV shows like *Emily in*

Paris. Meaning, then, can arise from both personal experience and from pervasive forms of mediation and storytelling.

Sense of place can also arise from a general sense of liveliness – one that involves all the senses. Indeed, the word "sense" in sense of place refers to the ways our bodies relate to place – through vision, sound, smell, taste, and touch, as well as through kinesthetic movement in place. A location with a sense of place is one that engages us sensorially. For this reason, an open-air market with all of its scenes, smells, and sounds seems to have more of a sense of place than a shopping mall, which seems comparatively antiseptic despite (or because of) the attempts at producing food courts, clouds of artificial scent, and the like. Repeated performances of bodies moving through space also create temporally variable senses of place – what geographer David Seamon called "place-ballets."[2] Locations with deep and shared senses of place can be richly choreographic, while those without them seem kinetically dead. A place with a rich sense of place is one that both engages the senses and has a certain liveliness. A place with no or little sense of place is stereotypically antiseptic, sterile, and dead. These are often described as "placeless" or "non-places."[3] These places–airports, service stations, hospitals, shopping malls, etc.–clearly have locations. They are somewhere, just like any other place. They also have locales – material shapes and forms within which the busyness of life takes place. Terms like placelessness and non-place, then, seem to refer to a lack of a sense of place or, perhaps, a sense of place that is so ubiquitous and repeated that it seems like it could be anywhere. More precisely perhaps, a term such as placeless refers to certain kinds of places that have senses of place we do not approve of. It is a term freighted with aesthetic and moral judgment. The presence of a sense of place is most often seen as a positive value. It is readily associated with the current investment in slowness and harking to tradition and authenticity – the kind of lifeways associated with the slow city (Cittaslow) movement and its headquarters in Orvieto, Italy. It advertised a conference on slow tourism in 2012 as one that "aims to exalt sense of place and identity and allows the tourist to criticise implicitly other tourist opportunities offered by the market."[4] The observation that some kinds of places have weak senses of place while other, slow, authentic, sites have deep senses of place neglects the fact that the same location, and the same material structures, can have different senses of place for different people. A place I may find sensually rich in a positive way may be forbidding and threatening for people who do not share my gender, skin color, income, or education. The opposite is also likely to be true.

The "sense" in sense of place also refers to a more general feel of place–a way of thinking and feeling–a way a place "makes sense." Sense, here, seems to be definite but also vague. Present, but mysterious. It is something that resists quantification. Orvieto is said to have it, while "other tourist opportunities offered by the market" do not. For place-makers, particularly those intentionally attempting to produce new places, or reconfigure old ones, this has sometimes looked a lot like branding or marketing. We can locate a place in an ideal location, and we can build buildings, public spaces, and infrastructure, but it is harder–I would argue–to engineer sense. Even if we could, we would have to ask whose sense was being catered to.

The idea of places being sites of sensory experience and the idea of an overall sense of place are often linked. In work I did regarding the erasure of the old Maxwell Street market in Chicago, for instance, observers over more than 100 years accounted for the place through reference to sight, sound, and smell.[5] North America's largest open-air market clearly had a sense of place. Positive accounts, such as that of Simone de Beauvoir following a visit in 1947, reveled in the sights and sounds of the market.

> Superstitions, science, religion, food, physical and spiritual remedies, rags, silks, popcorn, guitars, radios – what an extraordinary mix of all the civilizations and races that have existed throughout time and space. In the hands of merchants, preachers, and charlatans, the snares sparkle and the street is full of the chatter of thousands of brightly feathered birds.[6]

As the city government, developers, and the nearby University of Illinois at Chicago sought to take over the space for a new "urban village," athletics fields, and parking lots, a narrative of a failed place developed that also centered on the senses – often picking out the smellscape for particular attention. A report in the *Chicago Sun-Times* in 1977, for instance, noted "On Sunday, Maxwell Street will be filled with the smells of cooking food, the steamy smells of hot dogs and sharp tang of frying onions. But on this day it just smelled of the sour garbage that lay uncollected in the gutter."[7] Over time, accounts linked sensory geographies of visual disorder, unwanted odor, and cacophonous noise with narratives of decay and criminality to lay the groundwork for demolition and a new round of place-making that simultaneously erased the place that was already there. The evidence of the senses was used to create a negative sense of place that was the precondition for the production of a new sense of place more friendly to the desires of the city government, capital, and the university.

One way a sense of place develops, then, is through narratives of decay. Places can become stigmatized with deeply sedimented negative senses of place. This often happens in areas of cities associated with low-income people, and, particularly, Black and Brown people. This was the case for Maxwell Street. Stories of broken windows and rates of crime contribute to a sense of a place as subject to "urban decay." Geographer Tom Slater has argued that what he calls "territorial stigmatization" is part and parcel of the cycles of urban disinvestment and reinvestment that are necessary for the circulation of capital and production of profit in the urban environment.[8] This, in turn, leads to claims for the necessity of "urban renewal" or, in today's terms, place-making. When this cycle reaches its next stage, we are presented with seemingly successful examples of place-making. The Urban Design Lab suggests that successful examples include Manhattan's High Line, built on disused railway infrastructure, and Granville Island in Vancouver.[9] I have to admit I enjoy both of these places precisely because they are meant to appeal to people like me, a White man from the Global North with a reasonable income. I feel perfectly at home in each of those places. I cannot help but feel, however, that most other people in these places when I have visited seem an awful lot like me. I doubt if other people, who are less like me, would experience the same sense of place, or even visit in the first place. It is far from clear how the notion of sense of place can deal with difference. How might we think of places as having senses of place that are open to the world and the mobilities of people, things, and ideas that pass through them in what geographer Doreen Massey called a "progressive sense of place."[10]

While sense of place is most often a term used in a very positive way–linked to notions of attachment and care–it can have very negative consequences. Places do not have a sense in any essential way. Senses of place are produced every bit as much as the material structures of a locale are produced. They are also contested. In any place-making exercise, what is often overlooked is that the place in which such place-making occurs is already a place, to which people have become attached. Place-making always starts with a place that already exists. This makes place-making different than other kinds of making that start with a blank slate and some key components and tools. Any act of place-making is, by necessity, an act of place-erasure. One set of sensory experiences will be replaced by another, and, necessarily, one kind of overall sense will be replaced by another. In this process, the humanistic qualities of sensorial experience become inescapably matters of spatial justice.

1 Yi-Fu Tuan, *Space and Place: The Perspective of Experience* (University of Minnesota Press, 1977).

2 D. Seamon, "Body-Subject, Time-Space Routines, and Place-Ballets," in A. Buttimer & D. Seamon (eds), *The Human Experience of Space and Place* (Croom Helm, 1980), 148–65.

3 Marc Auge, *Non-Place: An Introduction to Supermodernity* (Verso, 2009).

4 Cittaslow, "Cittaslow: The Value of Slowness for the Tourism of the Future," https://www.cittaslow.org/news/orvieto-orvieto-i-cittaslow-value-slowness-tourism-future (accessed November 24, 2023).

5 Tim Cresswell, *Maxwell Street: Writing and Thinking Place* (University of Chicago Press, 2019).

6 Simone de Beauvoir, "America Day by Day (L'Amerique au jour le jour)," in Steven Conn & Max Page (eds), *Building the Nation: Americans Write About Their Architecture, Their Cities, and Their Landscape* (University of Pennsylvania Press, [1954] 2003), 69.

7 Roger Simon, "Capturing Song of Maxwell St.," *Chicago Sun-Times* (September 10, 1977).

8 Tom Slater, "Territorial Stigmatization: Symbolic Defamation and the Contemporary Metropolis," in John Hannigan & Greg Richards (eds), *The Sage Handbook of New Urban Studies* (Sage, 2017), 111–25.

9 Urban Design Lab, "Placemaking in Urban Design," https://urbandesignlab.in/placemaking-in-urban-design/ (accessed November 24, 2023).

10 Doreen Massey, "Power-Geometry and Progressive Sense of Place," in Jon Bird et al. (eds), *Mapping the Futures: Local Cultures, Global Change* (Routledge, 1993), 59–69.

Previous Left: Maxwell Street Market, Chicago, Illinois, 1977.

Previous Right: Google Earth Street view (Landsat /Copernicus), 07/2018.

ALEXA WEIK VON MOSSNER

SENSING IMAGINARY

Alexa Weik von Mossner is an associate professor of American studies at the University of Klagenfurt, Austria, and currently a visiting professor of Media and Culture Studies at the University of Freiburg, Germany. She explores contemporary environmental culture in both her research and her fiction. You can find her work at https://www.alexaweikvonmossner.com.

+ FILM STUDIES, COGNITIVE LITERARY STUDIES

In one of the most captivating sequences in Spike Jonze's science-fiction drama film *Her*, viewers follow Theodore Twombly [Joaquin Phoenix] as he travels across a near-future Los Angeles that could not be more different from the dark, rain-soaked urban landscapes they might remember from Ridley Scott's *Blade Runner* and other dystopian films.[1] Newly in love with the sentient operating system on his computer, Theodore is downright exuberant as he prances through the complex network of LA's sophisticated subway system and then triumphantly soars back up to the sunny surface at Dockweiler State Beach, taking a deep breath as he looks out on the Pacific Ocean.

Of course, this subway station does not exist in contemporary Los Angeles, and nor do most of the subway lines or any of the wide skywalks that Theodore traverses over the course of the story. As film critic Colin Marshall explains in his 2015 video essay on *Her,* the film's speculative geography combines selected shots from contemporary Los Angeles with those of a "sanitized Shanghai" to create a densely urbanized space surrounded by pristine nature in which cars are rare and all of Theodore's movement is done on foot, on sailboats, or on trains.[2] The reduced emissions do not seem to have done much for the hazy, yellowish skies we see throughout the film, in part because it is deliberately rendered in a reduced palette of strikingly warm colors, and in part because "what the audience is to imagine as being the LA of the future is in fact the Shanghai of the present," with much of the film shot in the Chinese metropolis.[3]

Although *Her* never explicitly draws attention to its speculative urban landscape, it is an integral part of the film's imaginary world. To feel lonely in such a utopian setting, Spike Jonze has said at a press conference, "is kind of even worse because it is a world where you should be getting everything you need, seemingly."[4] And yet, it is loneliness and the looming divorce from his estranged wife that leads Theodore to fall for the artificial intelligence and emotional attention of an operating system. Like his nonhuman and disembodied love interest, the film's imaginary lifeworld challenges viewers to ponder the nature of human perception, sensing, and emotion.

In *The Landscapes of Utopia*, Tim Waterman argues that "people inhabit their lifeworlds as much through the direct

LANDSCAPES

experience of the senses as they do through the imaginary constructs that they, as individuals and members of collectives and cultures, project into those worlds."[5] This makes sense from a neuroscientific point of view since, as neurologist Antonio Damasio has shown, the human brain processes direct perception, imaginary perception, and remembered perception in much the same way.[6] However, as Waterman also points out, "at a time of environmental crisis, when altering lifeworlds and life practices everywhere across the planet is crucial to the continued flourishing of our species and all others, it is vital to question the ways in which practices have been imagined."[7] This is where speculative work, be it fiction or nonfiction, can make important contributions to societal discourse and practice by dreaming up imaginary lifeworlds–*storyworlds*, as narrative theorist David Herman has called them–and inviting audiences to immerse themselves in them.[8] But how do such storyworlds come to live in the embodied minds of readers and viewers? How exactly, that is, do creators enable audiences not only to understand and envision the imaginary lifeworlds presented to them, but also to imagine *all* their sensual dimensions? Cognitive econarratology can shed some light on these questions.

In *Affective Ecologies*, I developed an approach that draws on research in affective science, cognitive literary and film studies, and the environmental humanities to highlight the central role of a process that neuroscientist Vittorio Gallese has called "embodied simulation" in the imaginary creation of narrative presence – the sense of having physically entered a tangible environment.[9] Involving the mirror neuron system, embodied simulation is a process that enables readers and viewers to imagine the sight, scent, sound, and "feel" of imaginary places in ways that are deeply visceral and emotional. Even more importantly, our memories of such imaginative perceptions can be durable and even stay with us for a lifetime. "Whether we experience events in real life, watch them in a movie, or hear about them in a story," explains psychologist Jeffrey Zacks, "we build perceptual and memory representations in the same format."[10] There are thus many commonalities in how human brains process and remember actual events and the imaginary events they encounter in film and literature, but there are also some interesting differences, not least when it comes to the question of sensual perception.

Cognitive narratologist Patrick Colm Hogan draws on Damasio's clinical research to develop a perceptual account of emotion in literary reading.[11] He argues that our affective response to a literary text is determined by emotional memories we have retained of previous experiences (real and imagined) and by the vivacity of the things we imagine while reading. For a definition of *vivacity,* Hogan looks to Elaine Scarry, who argues that it "comes about by reproducing the deep structures of perception."[12] What is simulated in literary reading, argues Scarry, "is not only the sensory outcome (the way something looks or sounds or feels beneath the hands) but (also) the actual structure that gave rise to the perception; that is, the material conditions that made it look, sound, or feel the way it did."[13] There are at least two features, then, that enable readers to experience what Scarry calls "non-actual, mimetic perception": one is a vivid account of *sensory outcomes*; the other is the evocation of the *material conditions* that give rise to those outcomes.[14] Let us look at an example to illustrate the difference and how the two features complement each other.

The protagonist of Kim Stanley Robinson's ecotopian novel *Pacific Edge* is a builder and architect as well as a city council member for the Green party in the town of El Modena, California.[15] Kevin Claiborne spends much of his days rehabilitating older houses to make them more energy efficient and ecologically sustainable, while his work in the city council lands him in a fierce battle to save the last undeveloped hilltop in El Modena from commercial development. Together with a group of volunteers, he also uses picks and shovels to reshape the urban landscape physically:

> Dirt flew into hoppers, picks hit stones with a *clink clink clink*, voices chattered with the week's gossip. They were tearing out the street. It had been a large intersection: four-lane asphalt streets, white concrete curbs, big asphalt parking lots and gas stations on the corners, shopping centers behind. Now the buildings were gone and most of the asphalt, too, hauled away to refineries in Long Beach; and they dug deeper.[16]

Narrated from a third-person perspective, this short passage includes both an account of sensory outcomes and

THE FLANKS OF BLUE FOOTHILLS
REVEALED THE ETCHING OF EVERY
RAVINE AND BENEATH THE FOOTHILLS
STRETCHING TO THE SEA, THE BROAD
COASTAL PLANE SEEMIN

THE COASTA
BUT TREETOPS

THEODORE
Respond later.
Email from
weather.
partly--
Delete.
LYWOOD

LYWOO
TEXT VOICE
Email from Amy: Hey Theodore,
Lewman's having a bunch of people
over this weekend. Let's all go
together. I miss you. I mean, not
EXT. LOS A
Slightly in
with massive
city designed
crowded and de
as the eye can
on Theodore wal
THE FLANKS OF BLUE FOOTHILLS
REVEALED THE ETCHING OF EVERY
RAVINE AND BENEATH THE FOOTHILLS
STRETCHING TO THE SEA THE BROAD
COASTAL PLAIN
coastal plain

TEXT VOICE
Email from Amy: Hey Theodore,
Lewman's having a bunch of people
over this weekend. Let's all go
together. I miss you. I mean, not
the sad, mopey you - the old, fun
you. Let's get him out. Gimme a
shout back. Love, Amy.
THE COASTAL PLAIN

EXT. LOS ANGELES STREET - DUSK
Slightly in the future
with massive office,
city designed
FOOTHILLS
OF EVERY
THE FOOTHILLS
THE BROAD

the evocation of the material conditions that give rise to those outcomes. The first sentence cues readers to imagine both visual and aural perception as it invites them to picture the material conditions ("dirt flew into hoppers"; "picks hit stones") as well as the sound this produces as the sensory outcome ("*clink clink clink*"). Moreover, readers are cued to perceive *motion*, which, according to Gabrielle Starr, "is often at the heart of the multisensory nature of imagery" because "vision allows for (and in sighted persons is preparatory to) motion."[17]

The question of "who perceives all this?" is also an interesting one in the above passage; it might either be the protagonist, Kevin, or the narrator. In either case, however, the reader is invited to share the perceiver's sensual experience by imagining the clinking sounds made by the picks as they hit stone. Following this brief scene of what is happening on the street, the narrator moves from showing into telling mode as he explains what it is that Kevin and his friends are "tearing out": a large intersection. It is a moment of *cognitive estrangement* that is typical for (environmental) science fiction and thus a sudden incongruence that might trigger an insight or even enlightenment.[18] While tearing out intersections may not necessarily be considered a good thing in readers' contemporary world, it is in Kevin's ecotopian future because there are hardly any cars left and people want more green space instead of streets.

Unlike Spike Jonze's cinematic vision of a hyper-urbanized LA, which adds thousands of high-rise buildings to the city's skyline, Robinson's literary evocation focuses on its periphery and *subtracts* buildings, streets, and other infrastructure, making it live up to its name again, Orange County:

> The flanks of the blue foothills revealed the etching of every ravine, and beneath the foothills, stretching to the sea, the broad coastal plain seemed nothing but treetops: groves of orange, avocado, lemon, olive; windbreaks of eucalyptus and palm; ornamentals of a thousand different varieties, both natural and genetically engineered.[19]

Once again, we do not know for certain who perceives this lush green landscape, since Kevin is only added to the scene a few sentences later. But *someone* is perceiving it, and readers are invited to share the perception imaginatively.[20] However, literature can also evoke a character's imagined or remembered perception, as in this passage, which introduces readers to Kevin's work:

> He enjoyed most of the labor involved in construction, especially the carpentry. All of it, really. The direct continual results of his efforts, popping into existence before his eyes: framing, wiring, stucco, painting, tilework, trim, they all had their pleasures for him. And as he did the designs for their little team's work, he also had the architect's pleasure of seeing his ideas realized...bringing the vision into material being.[21]

In this passage, rendered in free indirect discourse by a third-person narrator who gives readers access to Kevin's consciousness, readers are invited to simulate his reflections on his work from the moment of conception (and thus imagination) to the moment of materialization. For readers, however, it is *all* a matter of guided imagination as they follow what Marco Caracciolo has called an "instruction manual" for mental composition.[22] Ultimately, that is what storytelling is, but it is up to individual readers (or listeners) in what way their imagination *uses* these instructions. How much mimetic detail they need to be able to simulate the perceptual feel of a storyworld depends on their previous experience and related memories. An architect or builder might need less information to imagine the perceptual feel of "framing, wiring, stucco, painting, tilework, trim" than someone who has never worked with these materials. However, we all need *some* information, and it is the author's job to decide how much detail to provide.

As someone who also writes fiction, I know how challenging it can be to create imaginary landscapes for readers to inhabit with all their senses. Suzanne Keen has written about the importance of the author's empathy in the creation of characters, but it also takes empathy to create an imaginary landscape in a way that is convincing for readers – and enticing.[23] One of the characters in my novel, *Fragile*, is a landscape architect who specializes in creating sustainable rooftop gardens in the trying climate of a future New York.[24] Describing his designs was a challenge because it not only involved evoking a garden, but also the technical side of how that garden could survive in 120-degree weather. Once I had come up with the technical part, I had to decide how much of it I wanted to explain and how much I wanted to convey via the sensual effect it had on someone standing in the garden. The modeling and inhabitation of storyworlds, argues econarratologist Erin James, "is an inherently environmental process, in which readers come to know what it is like to experience a space and time different from that of their reading environment."[25] I have found this to be very true also for me as an author as I dream up a possible future world. In the most enjoyable moments of the writing process, I feel transported into that world, deeply immersed and apparently able to experience it with all my senses.

The process of imagined perception works somewhat, but not entirely differently in film, which can be directly perceived with the visual and aural sense but not with any other (although there have been attempts to make that possible). Importantly, the multimodality of visual imagery also holds true here. Gallese explains that "it encompasses the activation of somatosensory, emotion-related and motor brain networks."[26] Not only can images "make you sweat," but the multimodality of vision also allows for the activation of a range of other physical responses. This is why directors can use the visual look of a film to affect how viewers experience it on a sensual level. In Jonze's *Her*, the persistently warm color palette suggests pleasant weather, but it also highlights the diminished presence of green (spaces) in its utopian vision of Los Angeles.

A much greater presence of natural vegetation within a futuristic urban space can be found in films such as *Tomorrowland* or *Black Panther*.[27] Vancouver's former chief planner Brent Toderian has gone so far as to suggest that *Black Panther*'s Wakanda can be a conversation starter among landscape architects and city planners since its streets are primarily devoted to pedestrians and the architecture is organic, diverse, and regional, overgrown by hanging gardens.[28] While these elements can all be found in contemporary urban spaces, they are scaled to something much more spectacular that can be experienced on an imaginary level. As Carl Abbott notes in *Imagining Urban Futures,* such optimistic visions "often start with the physical rather than the social city, letting design take flight," but some such designs also aim to evoke more ecological, equitable, and sustainable ways of being in the world.[29] An understanding of imagined perception is therefore productive not only for the analysis of (science) fiction, but also for landscape architects who create, and then communicate, their own visions of future environmental designs.

1 *Her*, directed by Spike Jonze (2015); *Blade Runner*, directed by Ridley Scott (1982).

2 Colin Marshall, "Los Angeles, the City in Cinema: *Her* (Spike Jonze, 2013)," *YouTube* (2015), https://www.youtube.com/watch?v=GwZxsP2zLTE.

3 Jessica Ellicott, "China, Hollywood and Spike Jonze's *Her*," 4:3 (May 22, 2014), https://fourthreefilm.com/2014/05/china-hollywood-and-spike-jonzes-her/.

4 NYFF51: "Her" Press Conference | Spike Jonze, Joaquin Phoenix, Amy Adams, Rooney Mara, Olivia Wilde, https://www.youtube.com/watch?v=ZACOU3H5KO8.

5 Tim Waterman, *The Landscapes of Utopia: Writings on Everyday Life, Taste, Democracy, and Design* (Routledge, 2022), 2.

6 Antonio Damasio, *Descartes' Error: Emotion, Reason, and the Human Brain* (Vintage, 1994).

7 Waterman, *The Landscapes of Utopia*, 2.

8 David Herman, "Storyworld," in David Herman, Manfred Jahn & Marie-Laure Ryan (eds), Routledge *Encyclopedia of Narrative Theory* (Routledge, 2005), 569.

9 On affective ecologies, see Alexa Weik von Mossner, *Affective Ecologies: Empathy, Emotion, and Environmental Narrative* (Ohio State University Press, 2017); on embodied simulation, see Vittorio Gallese, "Mirror Neurons and Art," in Francesca Bacci & David Melcher (eds), *Art and the Senses* (Oxford University Press, 2011), 441. See also Anežka Kuzmičová, "Presence in the Reading of Literary Narrative: A Case for Motor Enactment," *Semiotica* 189 (2012), 24; Federico Pianzola, Giuseppe Riva, Karin Kukkonen & Fabrizia Mantovani, "Am I present in Imaginary Worlds? Intentions, Actions, and Flow in Mediated Experiences and Fiction," *Behavioral and Brain Sciences* 45 (2022).

10 Jeffrey M. Zacks, *Flicker: Your Brain on Movies* (Oxford University Press, 2015), 110.

11 Patrick Colm Hogan, *Affective Narratology: The Emotional Structure of Stories* (University of Nebraska Press, 2011), 55.

12 Elaine Scarry, *Dreaming by the Book* (Princeton University Press, 2001), 9.

13 Ibid.

14 Ibid.

15 Kim Stanley Robinson, *Pacific Edge* (Tom Doherty, 1990), 2.

16 Ibid.

17 G. Gabrielle Starr, *Feeling Beauty: The Neuroscience of Aesthetic Experience* (MIT Press, 2013), 124.

"Projects have a context," writes Kirsten Bauer in her contribution to *250 Things a Landscape Architect Should Know;* "they need to be seen in sun and rain and crowds and at night and when you're lonely or feeling like a hard-arsed eco-warrior. Capture your experiences."[30] The complexity of those sensual experiences then gets transmitted, first, to an imaginary blueprint expressed in narrative and visual form and, second, hopefully, to an actual project, but the process does not stop there. "The transmission of a landscape project's spirit," writes Catherine Mosbach, "is defined as early as its conception and implementation" with the goal to "leave a sensitive impression for subsequent generations."[31] Landscape design starts with the sensual experience of a place that feeds into and spills over the imaginary realm, where an alternative vision takes shape that, ultimately, struggles into material form to be sensed, experienced, and enjoyed by others for generations to come. Occasionally, such designs may reach into the speculative space of the utopian, as is the case for solarpunk architecture, which, as Pascal Hogue notes, is "characterized by grand, swooping biophilic structures replete with vertical forests and solar panels" and evokes "a utopian future that might be mistaken for science fiction."[32] Although such creations have been criticized for their (over)reliance on generative artificial intelligence and a general lack of feasibility, they might sensitize our imagination for a more sustainable future. Science fiction scholar Tom Moylan notes that utopia "evokes a project, more precisely a praxis, of radical critique and totalizing betterment of reality for all of humanity, all of nature, all of the planet."[33] Creative speculations can give us a sense of what a better future might *feel* like.

18 Eric C. Otto, *Green Speculations: Science Fiction and Transformative Environmentalism* (Ohio State University Press, 2015).

19 Robinson, *Pacific Edge,* 3.

20 James Phelan has argued that narrators can be focalizers and thus perceivers. James Phelan, "Why Narrators Can Be Focalizers–and Why It Matters," in Willie van Peer & Seymour Chatman (eds), *New Perspectives on Narrative Perspective* (SUNY Press, 2001), 51.

21 Robinson, *Pacific Edge,* 45.

22 Marco Caracciolo, "Blind Reading: Toward an Enactivist Theory of the Reader's Imagination," in Lars Bernaerts, Dirk de Geest, Luc Herman & Bart Vervaeck (eds), *Stories and Minds: Cognitive Approaches to Literary Narrative* (University of Nebraska Press, 2013), 83.

23 Suzanne Keen, *Empathy and the Novel* (Oxford University Press, 2007).

24 Alexa Weik von Mossner, *Fragile: A Novel* (Elzwhere Press, 2023).

25 Erin James, *The Storyworld Accord: Econarratology and Postcolonial Narratives* (Nebraska University Press, 2015), xi.

26 Vittorio Gallese, "Bodily Framing," in Caroline Jones, David Mather & Rebecca Uchill (eds), *Experience: Culture, Cognition, and the Common Sense* (MIT Press, 2016), 4.

27 *Tomorrowland*, directed by Brad Bird (2015); *Black Panther*, directed by Ryan Coogler (2018).

28 Brent Toderian, cited in Marc Malkin, "The Real-Life Possibilities of *Black Panther*'s Wakanda, According to Urbanists and City Planners," *Architectural Digest* (February 8, 2018), https://www.architecturaldigest.com/story/the-real-life-possibilities-of-black-panthers-wakanda-according-to-urbanists-and-city-planners.

29 Carl Abbott, *Imagining Urban Futures: Cities in Science Fiction and What We Might Learn from Them* (Wesleyan University Press, 2016), 261.

30 Kirsten Bauer, "Be in the Landscape," in B. Cannon Ivers (ed.), *250 Things a Landscape Architect Should Know* (Birkäuser, 2021), 16.

31 Catherine Mosbach, "Transmission," in ibid., 140.

32 Pascal Hogue, "What Is Solarpunk Architecture and How Does It Fit into the Built Future?" *Architizer* (2022), https://architizer.com/blog/inspiration/stories/solarpunk-architecture-and-the-built-future/.

33 Tom Moylan, "Foreword," in Waterman, *The Landscapes of Utopia*, xi.

Opposite: *Her* film stills showing a future Los Angeles.

KRIS PAULSEN
MARTIAN

TIMESLIPS

Kris Paulsen is an associate professor in the Department of History of Art at The Ohio State University. She is the author of *Here/There: Telepresence, Touch, and Art at the Interface* (2017) and numerous articles and essays on contemporary art, new media, and information technology. In 2023, Paulsen curated the exhibition *Sarah Rosalena: In All Directions* at the Columbus Museum of Art and edited a catalog of the same title.

+ ART HISTORY, MEDIA STUDIES

Since the mid-1960s, we earthlings have been spying up close on our neighboring world: flying by, circling, crashing into, and later roving the dusty surface of Mars.[1] In recent years, especially since the 2012 and 2021 landings of NASA's still-active Curiosity and Perseverance rovers, we have been receiving transmissions that convey sensory information about this distant world. Looking at images of an alien place, a place where humans have never been, it is easy to get caught up in the weird time they capture. Hundreds of millions of miles away, multiple Mars rovers crisscross the planet's surface, acting as embodied surrogates for earthly scientists by seeing, hearing, touching, and even tasting and smelling this other world.[2]

The term "telepresence" tends to indicate sensory extension to a distant location in approximately real time. According to the pioneering new media artist Roy Ascott, telepresence is the experience of being simultaneously "both here and there," creating connections between distant spaces by telecommunications technologies.[3] Other early theorists of telepresence, such as computer scientist Marvin Minsky, used the term much more narrowly to indicate the experience of embodied, multi-sensory presence through the remote manipulation of robots.[4] By either definition, the multiple rovers that have crisscrossed our neighboring planet since the mid-1990s would certainly qualify, and the telepresent sensory experiences they deliver can situate us scientifically, aesthetically, and experientially on the surface of Mars.

Admittedly, however, the simultaneous "now" experienced in telepresence is always a bit stretchy and capacious. Lag time is an inherent aspect of communication, even if one perceives it as instantaneous. The further the information must travel, across cables or bouncing off satellites, the greater the delay and the more it disturbs the perceptual and functional possibilities of real time. A lagging phone call or satellite video connection might cause one to realize just how far and fast information travels. Controlling a rover on Mars, for instance, involves a 20-minute delay between receiving and returning a signal, making real-time control of the device from Earth impossible.[5] Yet this lack of correlation does nothing to diminish the awe-inspiring experience of embodied presence on another planet – of viewing images from an out-of-sync past.

Considering the inherent lag caused by long distances, telepresence could also be described as an experience of being simultaneously *now* and *then,* not just *here* and *there.* This temporal mismatch might be fractions of a second or a long, disorienting delay that materializes the scale of our actions and ambitions. Even Ascott, while swooning at the power of simultaneity in his early descriptions of networked telecommunications, describes the telepresent person as not just present in two places in the same moment but also, in that distributed doubling, "at once everywhere and nowhere," "out-of-body" in a "timeless sea."[6]

Telepresence is thus, more properly, an experience of a past that one often mistakes as the now. Leaning into the strange misalignments of time caused by long-distance telecommunication, I allow myself in this essay to get a bit speculative (and, perhaps, a bit weird) by adding the "non-yet"–the future–to the now and then of telepresence. In this essay, I am interested in speculative, slippery ideas: timeslips and slip streams and even clay slip, a material that is neither liquid nor solid, that smooths over gaps and seals separated entities together. Drawing upon science fiction literature, quantum physics, Indigenous cosmologies, and the beautiful and perplexing craft practice of the artist Sarah Rosalena, I wish to argue that the telepresent observer is indeed, as Ascott claims, in a "timeless sea": simultaneously here and there, now and then, nowhere and everywhere. As such, these sensory experiences give us glimpses not just of an out-of-sync past but of futures yet to come.

Timeslips

The title of this essay, "Martian Timeslips," pulls on a thread running through science fiction literatures about Mars that imagine the planet as a locus for weird time. Philip K. Dick originated the phrase in his 1964 book, *Martian Time Slip*, which is set on a colonized Mars. An Indigenous and recognizably human population has been dispossessed and indentured by earthly oppressors. The main drama focuses on homesteaders trying unsuccessfully to make the desert world as much like mid-century America as possible. It is not merely the climate and habitat that make life so different in this new world but also the prevalence of neuro-divergence among children born on Mars. Over the course of the novel, it emerges that the children are experiencing a kind of sped-up time and are living, as it were, in the future. Unsurprisingly, perhaps, land speculators and real estate developers become interested in these abilities and how the children might aid in securing a profitable future and maintaining the status quo by meddling in the distinctions between then, now, and not-yet.

Kim Stanley Robinson borrows Dick's phrase in his *Mars Trilogy* from the mid-1990s, an epic story of the first scientific settlements on Mars and the revolutions that come with international colonization and resource extraction. In Robinson's novels, the "timeslip" names not a psychological condition but an anomaly of Martian clock and calendar time produced by the attempt to stay in sync with Earth and the cadence of its day. The Martian day, or "sol," is almost 40 minutes longer than a day on Earth. To keep the settlement synchronized with the home world, the clocks in the novel stop at midnight each night for that duration, opening a span of unaccounted time, when the colony is no longer held to the conventions that govern life and law. The timeslip becomes a witching hour, where revolutionary and normally unthinkable things occur. While the colonizers attempt to enforce earthly logic, structures, and control of a new place, the timeslip produces a prolonged moment of freedom and indeterminacy where anything might happen.

Dick's and Robinson's views of the timeslip in connection with the exploration and neocolonial settling of Mars bring together ideas of glimpsing the future and opening an opportunity for changing what appears to be the inevitable course of history. Using the idea of the timeslip as a wedge, I want to open a space to think about weird time; loops and bends; repeating pasts and spiraling, speculative futures. I want to think about what–and when–one sees looking *at and from* Mars.

Past and Future Mars

On February 18, 2021, NASA's Perseverance Rover touched down on the dusty surface of Mars. It landed in an ancient lakebed, now known as the Jezero Crater, with a great fanning river delta cut into the iron red rock. About 3.6 billion years ago–roughly contemporaneous with Earth's own Archean Eon, when life first began to emerge–water rushed across a warm and wet planet. Now, in this cold and dim desert, Perseverance preforms its astro-biological mission guided by earth-bound scientists, searching for fossilized evidence of microbial life in the clay soils of the once-blue Red Planet.[7] NASA stated long-term goal for reaching Mars is not solely scientific discovery but "to foster and attract new commercial enterprise."[8] Presumably, this means settling

1 NASA's 1964 *Mariner 4* mission was the first successful fly-by of Mars and produced the first images of its surface. NASA, "Mariner 4," https://nssdc.gsfc.nasa.gov/nmc/spacecraft/display.action?id=1964-077A[accessed November 29, 2023]. In 1971, NASA's *Mariner 9* became the first satellite to orbit Mars. Later that year, the Soviets crashed several probes into Mars's surface. Since then, dozens of instruments have observed Mars, launched by multiple nations and space agencies.

2 Dave Lavery, NASA Curiosity Program Executive, quoted in Geraint Jones, "Mars Curiosity rover send 'sounds, sights and smells' back home," *The Guardian* (August 29, 2012), https://www.theguardian.com/science/blog/2012/aug/28/curiosity-rover-sounds-sights-smells-mars.

3 Roy Ascott, "Connectivity: Art and Interactive Telecommunications," *Leonardo* 24, no. 2 (1991): 116. I discuss this topic at length in my book: Kris Paulsen, *Here/There: Telepresence, Touch, and Art at the Interface* (MIT Press, 2017).

4 Marvin Minsky, "Telepresence," https://web.media.mit.edu/~minsky/papers/Telepresence.html (accessed November 27, 2023). Originally published in *Omni Magazine* (1980).

5 According to NASA, it "takes about 5 and 20 minutes for a radio signal to travel the distance between Mars and Earth, depending on planet positions." The 10-minute turnaround time would be the absolute minimum for a scientist to make an observation from rover data and then send a reply. Thus, rovers receive instructions in daily batches from their scientific teams, and then make autonomous decisions based on the end goal programmed by its earth-bound operators. See NASA, "Mars 2020 Mission Perseverance Rover: Communications," https://mars.nasa.gov/mars2020/spacecraft/rover/communications/; and NASA, "In-situ Exploration and Sample Return: Autonomous Planetary Mobility," https://mars.nasa.gov/mer/mission/technology/autonomous-planetary-mobility/ (accessed November 27, 2023).

6 Roy Ascott, "Art and Telematics," in Edward Shanken (ed.), *Telematic Embrace: Visionary Theories of Art, Technology, and Consciousness,"* (University of California Press, 2003), 199, 187.

7 NASA, "Searching for Life in NASA's Perseverance Mars Samples," NASA Science Mars Exploration Program (February 17, 2021), https://mars.nasa.gov/news/8863/searching-for-life-in-nasas-perseverance-mars-samples/.

8 National Aeronautics and Space Administration, *NASA's Journey to Mars: Pioneering Next Steps in Space Exploration* (NASA, 2015), 1, https://www.nasa.gov/sites/default/files/atoms/files/journey-to-mars-next-steps-20151008_508.pdf.

the land, extracting valuable metals and minerals, and eventually terraforming this new world into green Earth's image.

No human has yet set foot on Mars, but Perseverance and NASA's other autonomous or semi-autonomous craft on Mars, such as Sojourner (1997), Spirit (2004–2010), Opportunity (2004–2018), Curiosity (2012–), and Ingenuity (2021–), allow one to imagine what it might be like. Their cameras take video and trace circular panoramas in the barren landscape, showing scattered fields of meteorites, broken volcanic debris strewn before steep craggy cliffs, and rising, rusty escarpments. The pale peachy sky hugs a horizon that appears alarmingly close on this significantly smaller world. The rovers deliver first-person views of a wilderness that is empty, disorderly, and dead. The scenes would be desolate and alienating if they were not so familiar: these otherworldly landscapes look like uncanny glimpses of the spectacular canyons of the American Southwest. NASA scientists named the area surrounding the landing site after Canyon de Chelly (or *Tséyí*) in the center of the Navajo Nation in Arizona, one of the longest continually inhabited places in North America.[9] For more than 5,000 years, various peoples and cultures, alongside even more ancient plant and animal residents, have shaped, groomed, farmed, and altered the landscape.[10] It is the utter random disorder of Mars—seemingly not a rock has been overturned or purposefully shoved aside—that signals humanity's radical distance from the images of this place, despite the rovers' embodied vantage points.

Videos and photographs from Mars force one to conceptualize a nature insulated from associations with anything living, wet, or moving with agency and the selfish desire to survive. This, however, is changing: the telepresent views provided by the rovers already bear human traces and index the drive to survive—to persevere—against all obstacles and odds. On the 401st day of its mission, Perseverance spotted an object off in the middle distance, framed by an epic stretch of windswept mountains and rolling dunes. A white anomaly lay on the sandy brown ground, obscured by dark rocky ejecta. An aerial view from another rover, the helicopter Ingenuity, revealed the object as Perseverance's own discarded parachute and 4.5 m diameter backshell. While Perseverance's mission is to acquire data about Mars and a world where life could have emerged, its images often narcissistically capture its own crisscrossing tire tracks and document an increasingly marked and disturbed—even littered—environment. Everywhere it ventures, Perseverance leaves neatly cut, perfectly cylindrical boreholes as it collects samples for a future return to Earth. These curious holes will remain long after wind erases the tire tracks and even the landing gear is pulverized to rust and dust.

Perseverance is the first rover with the explicit task of searching for life. It has already found undeniable evidence, but it is not the hypothesized fossilized microbes or primordial algae mats (at least, not yet); rather, it is the traces of human presence—even if at a distance—already scattered about the globe in advance of our bodily arrival. The age of the Anthropocene has dawned on Mars. When probing the ancient rocks of Mars, areologists are not only decoding the story of a past but are beginning to write a future.

Mars's present provides insight into the Earth's deep past, perhaps frozen at the moment just when or just before life could emerge. On Mars's surface, one might read the story of Earth's own geological and biological past, which has been written over by eons of action and events. But NASA's images and research also provide glimpses of Earth's possible future: one sees evidence of incomprehensible shifts in climate and atmospheric deterioration that have made the planet utterly different from the geological past it records. Written in the rock is the story of a place, once wet and wild with geological and atmospheric activity, that has been stilled and quieted. At the same time, the images reveal a place similar enough to our own that it is easy to fantasize how it could have a different future, shaken awake from its stasis. Indeed, it already looks like a place that humans could inhabit. One can imagine standing in these first-person perspectives, turning the world-making and world-breaking skills honed at home–thickening the atmosphere, raising global temperature–upon this other, unsuspecting world, making it over in Earth's image. One could loop back on Mars's timeline, warming the frozen water and rewinding to a previous moment in its environmental history.

Silicon Valley moguls such as Elon Musk and Jeff Bezos look to Mars as a potential solution to the climate crisis on Earth.[11] Rather than rehabilitate Earth's ecosystems, abandon fossil fuels and destructive forms of mining, develop carbon sinks, or invest in sustainable farming and architecture, these visionaries double down on damaging, extractive practices on Earth to transform Mars, rewinding its past to make it our potential future. These are dystopian dreams that imagine our world as so irrecoverable that investment and revolutionary science flee toward the stars.

Spiral Time

Yet there are weirder times at work in these images of Mars than in those of geological deep time and entrepreneurial forecasting. Our telepresent endeavors on Mars suggest other strange (but not impossible) temporalities that might allow one to imagine a break from these scientific and corporate narratives. Over the last two centuries, theoretical physics has revealed that time is not as simple as it may seem: it only appears to move in a straight line, from a fixed past through a shared present now and toward a yet-to-be-determined future. This is a distortion produced by our particular, situated perspectives in the grand cosmic, quantum universe.[12] An event, quantum physicist Carlo Rovelli writes, may occur both before and after another one. I will take the provocation that time may be otherwise–in a great simultaneous block or less linearly ordered or jumping here and there–to blur apparently stable pasts and to speculate upon seemingly impossible futures. Doing so opens the possibility of revisioning, reinventing, or reclaiming our apparent now and its political vectors as so forcefully determined by Silicon Valley. At the center of this swirl, I place the artwork of Sarah Rosalena, whose beautiful and perplexing objects use digital fabrication technologies, machine learning, NASA-generated research, and Indigenous craft practices to upend our stable apprehension of pasts, presents, and futures.[13]

While potentially outlandish and self-consciously science fictional, the temporalities I suggest in relationship to Rosalena's work are not novel. Anishinaabe literary scholar Grace Dillon has theorized a comparable concept of spiraling time that she calls "native slipstream," which uncovers quantum logics in traditional thought and storytelling practices. Drawing upon a broad range of Indigenous science fiction literatures and cosmological beliefs, Dillon suggests nonlinear, non-Western conceptualizations of time that "infuse stories with time travel, alternate realities and multiverses, and alternative histories. As its name implies," she writes, "native slipstream views time as pasts, presents, and futures that flow together like currents in a navigable stream. It thus replicates non-linear thinking about spacetime."[14] As Dillon explains, this is an

9 The naming convention for features observed on Mars will be to match their likenesses to "national parks and preserves on Earth with similar geology." NASA, "NASA's Perseverance Mars Rover Mission Honors Navajo Language" (March 11, 2021), https://mars.nasa.gov/news/8886/nasas-perseverance-mars-rover-mission-honors-navajo-language/.

10 Archaeological evidence suggests Indigenous Americans have lived in the canyon for approximately 5,000 years through to contemporary Diné residents. National Parks Service, "Arizona: Canyon de Chelly National Monument," https://www.nps.gov/articles/dechelly.htm (accessed November 29, 2023).

11 See Christian Davenport, *The Space Barons* (Public Affairs, 2018).

12 Carlo Rovelli, *The Order of Time* (Riverhead Books, 2018), 81–94.

13 I have previously surfaced some of these ideas in a catalog essay for a mid-career survey of Rosalena's work that I curated, *In All Directions.* See Kris Paulsen (ed.), *Sarah Rosalena: In All Directions* (The Columbus Museum of Art, 2023).

14 Grace L. Dillon, "Imagining Indigenous Futurisms," in Grace L. Dillon (ed.), *Walking the Clouds: An Anthology of Indigenous Science Fiction* (University of Arizona Press, 2012), 3.

15 Dillon, "Imagining Indigenous Futurisms," 3.

16 Ibid., 4.

17 Grace L. Dillon & Pedro Neves Marques, "Taking the Fiction out of Science Fiction: A Conversation about Indigenous Futurisms," *e-flux journal* 120 (September 2021), https://www.e-flux.com/journal/120/417043/.

18 For example, Yusoff explains how Antarctic ice cores record the increase in carbon capture that resulted when the Indigenous population in the Americas was decimated in the wake of colonization in the 15th century. Kathryn Yusoff, *A Billion Black Anthropocenes or None* (University of Minnesota Press, 2018), 51.

19 See NASA's "3D Printed Habitat Challenge," https://www.nasa.gov/prizes-challenges-and-crowdsourcing/centennial-challenges/3d-printed-habitat-challenge/ (accessed November 28, 2023).

20 For an extensive analysis of science fiction's relationship to and dependence on colonialism, see John Rieder, *Colonialism and the Emergence of Science Fiction* (Wesleyan University Press, 2008).

21 As brilliantly described in Yusoff, *A Billion Black Anthropocenes or None*, 51.

ancient way of thinking that now appears futuristic, as it seems to "anticipat[e] cutting-edge physics [such as the multiverses of quantum mechanics], ironically suggesting that natives have had it right all along."[15] It is experimental and avant-garde, she argues, but nevertheless "models a cultural experience of reality" while also recovering "Native space of the past...to build better futures."[16] The native slipstream evokes ancient and traditional–yet simultaneously futuristic and radical–conceptions of temporality. Time, she writes, may be shaped more like a spiral, a shape which has the potential to rupture colonial frameworks and expectations, thereby producing a glimpse of the world outside of settler time.[17] Native slipstream is another kind of timeslip in which one can imagine alternative outcomes and new pathways that connect the future to the past without being stymied by the inertia of the now.

Even without veering into science fiction, Kathryn Yusoff's groundbreaking book, *A Billion Black Anthropocenes or None,* likewise suggests how the linear, sedimented geological record evidences a kind of looping time in which an anticipated and much-feared event has already occurred. The geological record provides proof of numerous prior apocalypses experienced by Black, Brown, and Indigenous peoples, in which civilizations have been eradicated and ecosystems destroyed by the acts and effects of settler colonialism.[18] One can see the slave trade, intercontinental colonialism, and racial capitalism written in rock and ice. Dillon's work echoes these statements, arguing that Indigenous peoples are already living in the post-apocalypse–the future that white liberal communities actively fear–and that it may be ancestral technologies and knowledges that shape the future.

Rosalena is an Indigenous Wixárika artist working at the intersection of computation and craft. She draws upon NASA's astronomical, geological, and remote sensing research to create objects that unsettle the apparent boundaries of past, present, and future while complicating other false binaries. Her ceramic series *Transposing a Form* (2020), for example, troubles the comfortable categorizations of handmade and autonomous, art and craft, earthly and otherworldly, human and more than human. Coil by coil, her sculptures appear to have grown into their spiraling shapes, like corals or sponges: those strange animals that often seem more like motionless plants or sedentary stones. They take spiral forms, familiar from ancient and enduring techniques that transform clay, the humblest of materials, into the useful tools that support and sustain civilizations. The precision of their layers recalls both the automated path of a 3D printer and the mathematical forms found in nature: the tight phyllotaxis of leaves on a succulent, the scales of a pinecone, the logarithmic expansion of a nautilus shell. The coiling technique simultaneously signals the traditional and the high-tech, the handmade and the mechanically produced. Of all the oppositions captured within these objects, one startles above all: these are not terra-cotta, or "baked earth" – rather, they claim to be baked Mars.

NASA's rovers view, observe, poke, probe, and burn with lasers so as to sniff and taste for us the mineral and chemical composition of Mars. The result of their investigations is Martian Regolith Simulant, the material from which Rosalena makes these structures. She uses a 3D printer, developed in collaboration with scientists at NASA's Jet Propulsion Laboratory, filled with Martian clay slip. These are time-bending objects: while the tight coils and materials are reminiscent of traditional earthen pots made in the American Southwest for millennia, MMS-2 (short for Mojave Mars Simulant 2) makes the two environments geological and chemical analogs. It

Opposite: Sarah Rosalena, *Transposing a Form*, 2020.

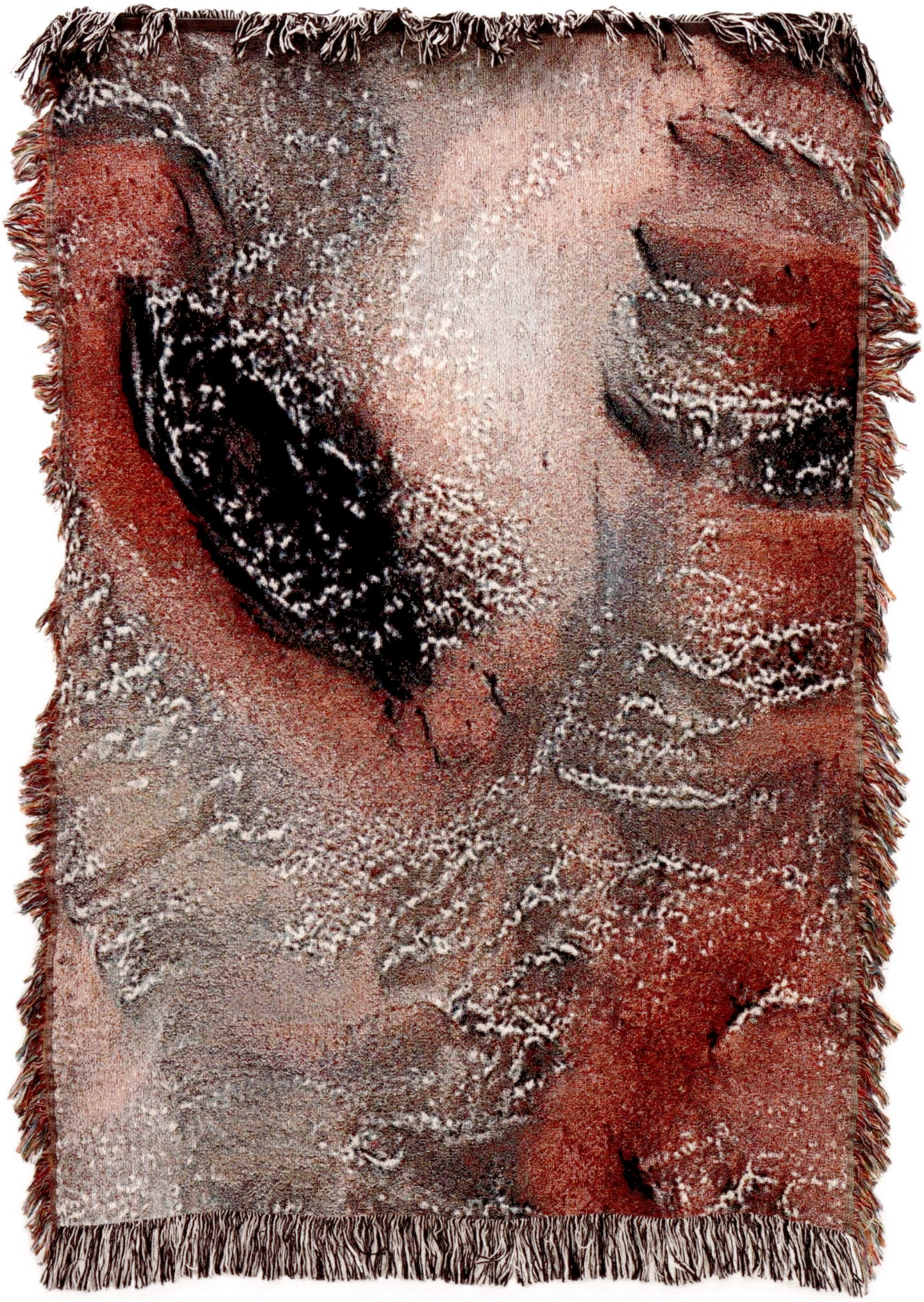

Sarah Rosalena, *Above Below*, 2020.

is likely that any future construction on Mars would be 3D printed from local adobe, making further strange connections between traditional Indigenous technologies and speculative human futures.[19] The long success of populations in desert climates, farming and thriving, are held up by scientists as models for sustainable lifeways in future off-world settlements. There is a deep and unpleasant irony in these loops, as technologies and knowledges once dismissed as primitive–and populations faced with unrelenting dispossession and genocide–are reclaimed by high technology and advanced research as visions of the future.

Rosalena's objects are unsteady in the now. They seem to oscillate between the past and the future in ways that cause one to see the analogies between colonial-era atrocities and futuristic entrepreneurial dreams of new frontiers, resource sites, and markets. They point to science fiction as a body of literature about manifest destiny, colonial expansion, and alien encounters; visions of the future are most often repeating, looping versions of a past.[20] The manifestation in our present of an artifact that appears to be from a possible future and that looks like something from the past destabilizes our hold on the now, introducing a wobble into the linear progression of space-time. This curve enables us to reimagine an approach and take a turn. We can enter the loop of a spiral rather than the vectors toward manifest destiny and extractive futures. Rather than predicting what craft might look like in a post-earth future, these objects turn our attention back to Earth, to the environments that space entrepreneurs are further damaging by imagining a destiny elsewhere. If ancestral practices seem to be the high-tech solutions to environmental challenges off-world, then surely they are also ways to imagine a future on a paradise planet we have defiled. Rather than looking to an imaginary future in which heroic humans show their perseverance and ingenuity playing scientist-gods on a dead world, Rosalena's work loops our attention back to the earth from which these simulants are made and to the opportunity to be stewards of the world at hand. This place might become captivating and mysterious again, turning our attention toward a past state as a future goal.

Rosalena's companion body of work, the Jacquard woven tapestries *Above Below* (2020), uses a neural network to process the epic amount of photographic satellite data collected from the Mars Reconnaissance Orbiter (2005–) to predict and visualize environmental and climate shifts on Mars over millions of years. She has trained the neural network, however, on historical data about Earth. She processes Martian data based on what we know about Earth, its deep past and the effects of human actions and interventions. These double-sided tapestries enable the viewer to toggle between pasts and futures. The recto shows a red planet turning blue; the verso shows just the opposite: a blue planet turning red. It is unclear where we stand in relationship to these images: in the deep past, the not-yet, or a strange, speculative, slippery now from which to turn in an alternate direction. Rosalena's tapestries, though written line by line on her loom, tell multiple stories with different beginnings and alternate trajectories toward the future by manifesting an unstable object materially in our present. They allow one to imagine the terraforming of Mars and, at the same time, the desertification and drowning of Earth through the ravages of climate change. There is a profound ambivalence and indeterminacy in the objects: a blue Mars is an image of its ancient past and a possible outcome of human intervention. A red Earth is, hopefully, a future that will never come, avoidable only through radical action in the present moment, rather than through fantasies of escape and starting anew. *Above Below* presents the viewer with a choice: if a blue Mars implies a red or uninhabitable

Earth, then our attention must turn from the stars and back toward the firm ground beneath our feet, leaving Mars to its own destiny.

While the Anthropocene fuels nightmares of impending ecological disaster and civilizational collapse, the perception of the apocalypse being in the future is a matter of perspective and racialized privilege.[21] To reinvest in Earth requires imagining ourselves into those remote yet embodied views of and from Mars that do not reveal it as an analog of Earth–one that could be remade through hard work and innovation–but that expose its utter difference. Entering the timeslip offers the potential to imagine something new for Earth: a destiny splintered off the apparently inevitable trajectory toward a future chosen by entrepreneurs. Living on Earth means committing to imagining different ways of being on and with the world, returning to underappreciated ancestral ways rather than imagining ourselves the same (colonizing, mining, conquering), only elsewhere. We might see in the timeslip a circumstance in which a landscape, on Earth or Mars, might have some rights and claims to sovereignty outside or even against human need and desire, where traditional knowledges alongside new innovations could rehabilitate current conditions by recognizing and respecting the destinies of non-human things. From Perseverance's telepresent position on Mars, one can step into the timeslip where now, then, and not-yet become unfixed and open to revolutionary change. The image we need from Mars is the one that looks back toward Earth.

IMAGE CREDITS

Endpapers

Allegory of the Sense of Smell by Jan Brueghel the Elder/ Peter Paul Rubens c. 1617-1618, public domain via Wikimedia Commons.

Editorial

p. 4: *The Five Senses*, illustration by Mads Berg. Used with permission.

Sense-Certainty, Identity, and the Reality Paradox

p. 6-7: Image by Devon Bruzzone using photographs by Dennis Hill (CC BY-2.0 Deed) and Thomas Schanz (CC SA 4.0, altered), used with permission.

p. 11: *Optical Illusion* (2008) by Micah Baldwin, used under CC BY-SA 2.0 via Flickr.com.

Tasting the Cure

p. 14: *Tsaghveri Efflloresence* by Sarah Coleman, used with permission (cropped).

p. 15: "Borjomi 1, oL" by Indre Borkomi, used under CC BY-SA 4.0 International via Wikimedia Commons.

p. 20: *Tsaghveri Spring* by Sarah Coleman, used with permission.

Color of Nature: Capitalism-Trained Eyes and the Visual Appetite

p. 22-23, 28-29: Images by Devon Bruzzone, used with permission.

Olfactory Sublime

p. 32-33: Image by Junyi Yang using prints from Cooper-Hewitt, Smithsonian Design Museum and thegraphicsfairy.com, used with permission.

p. 34-39: Drawings by Junyi Yang, used with permission.

Smell of Surveillance

p. 40: *Gum* by Joshua Ganderson, used under CC BY-2.0 Deed via Flickr.com (altered).

p. 44: *Stranger Visions* by Heather Dewey-Hagborg, used with permission.

Aquatic Living Sensors and the Making of Common Sense

p. 46: Image courtesy of Lauren and Simon Freeman of the PADRES Naval Undersea Warfare Center – Newport Division team, from https://www.darpa.mil/news-events/2020-09-28 (cropped).

p. 51: Image courtesy of NOAA National Marine Sanctuary of American Samoa (cropped).

Listening to Landscape

p. 52-57: Images by Junyi Yang, used with permission.

In Conversation with Mark Peter Wright

p. 58: *The Noisy Nonself or, I, the Thing in the Margins*, 2015, by Mark Peter Wright, used with permission.

Sensescapes

p. 64-71: Images by Lillia Schmidt, used with permission.

Sense of Smog

p. 72: *Smoggy Day in Los Angeles*, September 14, 1955. Courtesy of Los Angeles Public Library.

p. 76-77: *Smog Covers Downtown LA*, 1964. Photo credit: Mike Sergieff. Courtesy of Los Angeles Public Library.

Sensorimotor Acts

p. 80: Image by Wenshu Huang using *The Yellowstone River winds through wintry Yellowstone National Park in Wyoming* (Feb. 8, 2016) by Carol M. Highsmith, photographer, public domain (altered).

Deaf Experience: Beyond ADA Standards

p. 86: Image by Junyi Yang using WordCloud for Python by Andreas Mueller, used with permission.

p. 92: *Resting Conversations: Seats at the Table* by Raquel Meseguer Zafe and Helen Stratford, London Festival of Architecture, 2023. Photograph © Luke O'Donovan, used with permission (cropped).

Audible Cartographies of Power

p. 94: Image by Junyi Yang using *Turntable Arm* under CC0 1.0 Universal Public Domain Dedication license via pixabay.com (altered).

p. 98: Image by Chip Py, photographer, acquired by the People's Archive of the DC Public Library, used with permission.

Senses of Place

p. 100: Image by Wenshu Huang using Google Earth Street view (July 2018) and Jonas Dovydenas, photographer, *Maxwell Street Market, Chicago, Illinois*, Chicago Ethnic Arts Project collection (AFC 1981/004: b42184). Courtesy of Library of Congress American Folklife Center (cropped).

Sensing Imaginary Landscapes

p. 106-07: Images by Lillia Schmidt, used with permission.

p. 110: Film stills from *Her*, Spike Jonze, 2013, Warner Bros Pictures via Screemusings.org (unaltered).

Martian Timeslips

p. 112-13: *Perseverance's Selfie with Ingenuity* by NASA/JPL-Caltech/MSSS, public domain via mars.nasa.gov.

p. 118: Sarah Rosalena, *Transposing a Form,* 2020. Courtesy of Blum & Po, Los Angeles. Photo credit: Jenalee Harmon. Courtesy of the artist.

p. 120-21: Sarah Rosalena, *Above Below,* 2020. Courtesy of Blum & Po, Los Angeles. Photo credit: Jenalee Harmon. Courtesy of the artist.

IN THE NEXT ISSUE OF

LA+

The idea of "environment" is foundational to landscape architecture – as backdrop, as surround, as something to help. But what is *the* environment, or *an* environment? First and foremost, it is a word that is so pervasive–and its meaning taken for granted–that it is easily forgotten how recently the term has proliferated, particularly as a qualifier for myriad disciplines, institutions, and activities: environmental history, environmental studies, environmental science, environmental justice, environmental art, environmental planning, environmental protection, environmentalism. In our upcoming issue, **LA+ ENVIRONMENT**, designers and scholars illuminate the wide range of interpretations, histories, and projects that engage with this elusive idea.

CHRISTINA ANTIPORDA
DANIEL BARBER
ETIENNE BENSON
HOLLY JEAN BUCK
LINO CAMPRUBI BUENO
JESS CONARD
VINITA DAMODARAN
SONJA DÜMPELMANN
DIANA GUO
MARIA IVANOVA
RAMI KANAFANI
LAURA MARTIN
CHAD MONTRIE
MICHAEL OPPENHEIMER
MARCUS OWENS
MELISSA S. RAGAIN
JESSICA VARNER
ANDREW WITT

OUT **FALL 2025**